Praise for *BACK TO THE CUTTING BOARD*

"Christina's magical cooking secrets are at your fingertips. Glowing health and delicious recipes aside, embark on this journey to rekindle cooking bliss a.k.a. the art of cooking! With Christina as your guide, the stress associated with tackling a meal will be alleviated and replaced with curiosity, intuition, simplicity, and play. How awesome is that?"

ALICIA SILVERSTONE
AWARD-WINNING ACTRESS, BESTSELLING AUTHOR
OF *THE KIND DIET*, ANIMAL RIGHTS AND ENVIRONMENTAL
ACTIVIST, AND ENTREPRENEUR

"What Christina has written here is unlike any cookbook you've ever read. She presents a philosophy that uses the kitchen as a tool to allow you to connect with your true self. Yes, the recipes in here are delicious and can help you reclaim or optimize your health—and in Christina's case, they actually saved her life. But you will learn how to nourish not just your body, but your soul—by finding a deeper meaning in the so-called 'chore' of cooking. Grab your chef's knife and cutting board and get ready. You're not just going to cook. You're going on a journey."

CHEF ROBERT IRVINE

"Back to the cutting board? Gladly! This wonderful new book from Christina is full of excellent ideas that will make you fall in love with cooking again. If you have drifted from the kitchen, it will inspire you to get back to it. If you are new to cooking, then you couldn't ask for a better 'in.' Vegan cooking is having its moment and Christina's new book perfectly captures the spirit of what's happening in today's food world."

RICH LANDAU
CHEF/OWNER OF THE VEDGE RESTAURANT GROUP,
JAMES BEARD NOMINEE, AND BESTSELLING AUTHOR

"Most folks fear getting into the kitchen to cook for good reason; it can be daunting. But not when Christina Pirello is guiding us. In *Back to the Cutting Board*, Christina introduces the kitchen tools, gadgets, techniques, and ingredients as if they are old friends that have been patiently waiting to re-connect with us and nourish us. She shares many good reasons why it's essential that we get back inside the kitchen. And, once you're there . . . your body and mind will be deeply nourished by Christina's delicious recipes. Don't wait one more second! Open up this book, connect with your old friends (and yourself), and start cooking!"

ANDREA BEAMAN
CHEF, HERBALIST, AND AUTHOR OF *HAPPY HEALTHY THYROID*

"There is joy in Christina's cooking. Because her food isn't just delicious and beautiful. It's also wholesome in ways that draw you in, making you simply want to eat and be better. And her recipes make that easy."

J.M. HIRSCH
EDITORIAL DIRECTOR OF *MILK STREET MAGAZINE*

BACK TO THE
CUTTING
BOARD

*Luscious Plant-Based Recipes
to Make You Fall in Love (Again)
with the Art of Cooking*

CHRISTINA PIRELLO

BenBella Books, Inc.
Dallas, TX

BenBella

BenBella Books, Inc.
10440 N. Central Expressway, Suite 800
Dallas, TX 75231
www.benbellabooks.com
Send feedback to feedback@benbellabooks.com

Printed in the United States of America
10 9 8 7 6 5 4 3 2 1

Library of Congress Cataloging-in-Publication Data
Names: Pirello, Christina, author.
Title: Back to the cutting board : luscious plant-based recipes to make you
    fall in love (again) with the art of cooking / Christina Pirello.
Description: Dallas, TX : BenBella Books, Inc., [2018] | Includes
    bibliographical references and index.
Identifiers: LCCN 2018003618 (print) | LCCN 2018011486 (ebook) | ISBN
    9781946885487 (electronic) | ISBN 9781946885364 (trade paper : alk. paper)
Subjects: LCSH: Cooking (Natural foods) | Nutrition. | Vegan cooking. |
    LCGFT: Cookbooks.
Classification: LCC TX741 (ebook) | LCC TX741 .P5634 2018 (print) | DDC
    641.3/02—dc23
LC record available at https://lccn.loc.gov/2018003618

Cover and interior food photography: Maja Danica Pečanić (styling & photography), Vladimira
    Vlatka Frketić (food preparation), Ana Haberman/Tri lukne (ceramic artist)
Author photo by Carmine Silveroli
Editing by Trish Sebben Malone
Copyediting by Karen Levy
Proofreading by Kimberly Broderick and Sarah Vostok
Indexing by WordCo Indexing Services, Inc.
Text design and composition by Kit Sweeney Photography & Design
Front cover design by Oceana
Full cover design by Sarah Avinger
Printed by Versa Press

Distributed to the trade by Two Rivers Distribution, an Ingram Brand
www.tworiversdistribution.com

Special discounts for bulk sales (minimum of 25 copies) are available.
Please contact Aida Herrera at aida@benbellabooks.com.

TO JOHN DUFF

For changing my life and for unconditional
love, friendship, and support.

CONTENTS

INTRODUCTION

I come from a family of true food lovers. It seemed to me that every moment we celebrated, mourned, discussed, or marked was centered around a feast. We loved to eat as much as we loved to cook. The kitchen truly was the heart of our home, always fragrant with the perfumes of luscious food cooking. I was raised with a healthy respect for fresh food, spending countless hours with my father and grandfather in their gardens, picking and eating as they tenderly cared for their plants. When other kids were roller-skating on Friday nights, I was with my mother at the farmers market learning (reluctantly . . . I wanted to be roller-skating) how to pick a great tomato or melon.

As I grew, the passionate way my family communicated (translation: yelling) proved to be too much for me. I was deemed "sensitive" or "delicate"—a "wuss" by my brothers—because the noise of their boisterous conversations and debates would leave me jittery and nervous.

I noticed, though, that none of that drama crossed the threshold into the kitchen. In that fragrant room, people cooked and worked in perfect harmony, telling stories, laughing, smiling, sharing tips and ideas. No one was allowed to argue, cry, or create havoc in the kitchen. "Take it outside" was the refrain should any *senza senso* (nonsense) find its way into the room. The pure joy of that room, and the serenity and respect with which food was prepared, seduced me from the start. I didn't want to be anywhere else in the house, not when I could be in and around *this* . . . this quiet passion and happiness.

I asked my father to build me a step stool so I could reach the counter to learn more by watching and helping my mother, and I have never looked back from the stove. To this day, the kitchen is precious; cooking is my job, but I love every second of my time in this room. I look for excuses to "test a new recipe" when I just want to play with my food. I love developing recipes, creating beautiful presentations, cooking new and delicious combinations of food, and, of course, always discovering how the energy of food creates the dance of life.

I am still drawn in by the serenity of the kitchen and the deep peace and balance I find there. A hard day in business will be forgotten when I pick up my knife and head to the cutting board. I know, I know; it sounds a bit airy-fairy, but my sensitivity to noise helped me find my place in the world. My friends laugh at me when I say that I would spend all my time in the kitchen if I could.

In this modern world, where hands-on, from-scratch cooking has fallen by the wayside, it's amazing how much we think about, talk about, read about, and obsess about food. We watch other people cook food. We consider watching people decorate cupcakes to be scintillating television. As food writer Michael Pollan famously stated, we spend more time watching people cook than actually cooking. The question in my mind is: with all the cooking shows, studies, statistics, information, and data bombarding us daily, do we really understand food? I don't mean grams and vitamins and calories; we have that down to a science. But do we get it? I've seen very little in my life and work that leads me to believe that we are collectively connecting the dots between food and wellness. I think we are a great eating culture, but are we a true food culture?

Although we may have developed a deeper understanding of what is in the food we eat (we read labels and nutrition newsletters like novels), we appear to have forgotten why we eat. In my career as a teacher, I must have said, "You are what you eat" millions of times—it is even the opening line of my first cookbook, *Cooking the Whole Foods Way*. A cliché to be sure, but not without truth, as most clichés are.

Somewhere along the information highway, we got lost, and as a result, we seem to be always searching. Every self-help book that can find its way to a shelf becomes a best seller, proclaiming to have the answer. And we dutifully go on each quest . . . for our inner child, our authentic self, our true spirit. We trek off to groups; we write in our journals; we examine our deepest selves. And it seems that the more we struggle, the more the answers elude us. What are we missing? (You know the answer's coming, right?)

And then there are the diets. We've embraced low fat, high protein, low protein, high carbs, low or no carbs, grapefruit, cabbage soup, Paleo, and the Champagne and grape diet (which sounds like fun at least . . .). We weigh food, reconstitute food, drink chemical-laced shakes, eat energy bars, measure, and count portions. We measure food into colorful, various size containers, so we'll know when we've had our allowances of calories. I think there may be more diet programs than religious affiliations. Yet we just keep losing ground (and our wellness). We grow more miserable about it despite what we hear about body acceptance.

We head to the gym, so we can get on a treadmill instead of walking or running in nature. We take the elevator to the floor that houses the stair machines rather than walk the stairs. We bike on bikes that go nowhere. Now, I am an avowed gym rat, completely dedicated to lifting weights and sweating my way through boot camps and HIIT workouts. And that's great, but I never forget that Mother Nature is waiting for me to come outside and play. She's waiting for all of us to turn our faces to her brightly shining sun and bask in the light and fresh air.

Why? Because we are fundamentally products of nature, subject to the same laws that govern all living organisms. It's our natural home. But what makes us human is our unique ability to create what we visualize in our minds. Dogs don't build condos; cats aren't famous for highway construction. And therein lies part of the problem. We have become enchanted with our abilities to manifest our visions and are enslaved by the results. The sophisticated technology we've created and love so very much has alienated us from our true natures and insulated us from the essential life forces that nourish and create us. In setting ourselves against or outside of nature, we have created an imbalance, and in so doing, created conditions of physical, emotional, and spiritual malaise.

Look, I'm not just babbling on here about nature and flowers. There's a reason I can speak about this with some authenticity. I was breezing through life, thinking I was doing all the right things: recycling, exercising regularly, drinking diet soda like any good single woman. And then cancer hit me like a baseball bat to my skull. I was forced to reckon with my life and ultimately change . . . *everything* . . . dramatically. A diagnosis of stage four leukemia and an expiration date on my young life was not at all what I was expecting. My mother had just passed away from colon cancer and the family was still reeling. I remember thinking, as the doctor grimly explained my condition, that if I could just memorize the pattern in his carpet (gray with maroon fleur-de-lis), I wouldn't panic and run from his office screaming. This couldn't be happening. I was twenty-six years old and fit. I was a vegetarian. I *recycled*, for goodness' sake! It was so unfair.

I had no idea that I was receiving the greatest gift of my life.

I met (and later married) the man who would alter the course of my life forever. Robert took me by the hand and educated my "junk food vegetarian" brain about real nutrition and the philosophy of macrobiotics and plant-based eating. It was like nothing I had ever heard.

And I fell in love . . . with him, with life, and with this style of living and cooking. Almost from day one of my lifestyle reboot, I thought of the passion with which I now approached cooking, which I had always loved, but this . . . this was different. At first, my dedication and discipline (no other way to describe it) were to stave off the Grim Reaper, but as I cooked, I discovered this deeply satisfying joy in creating food that would manifest life and wellness. I felt deeply connected to nature. In a way, I felt like I was losing my mind. Who gets this seriously involved in their cooking? And vegetables, at that? But then I realized I wasn't losing my mind; I was gaining my sanity. I quickly lost my fear of death and illness; I knew that my fate was in my hands . . . and in my skillet.

Years ago, when I first discovered the kitchen, cooking with my mother and my crazy family (and loving it), someone gave me a copy of *The Joy of Cooking*. I didn't really get the idea, even though I cooked delicious recipes from this classic. But joy? Unbridled joy? Then I discovered I could cook vegetables, grains, and beans and restore health and wellness with some of the most delicious food I had ever cooked. *Yes! Yes! Yes! Yes! Yes!* (as Meg Ryan famously shouted in *When Harry Met Sally*).

I'm not a big fan of labels—macrobiotic, plant-based, vegan, vegetarian—as they all come with baggage. I have always referred to my style of cooking based on the feeling it evokes in me: passion. Plant-passionate cooking is exactly how it sounds. There's no hidden meaning or veiled philosophy. I am passionate about plants and all that they provide us.

As a result, I fell in love with everything to do with cooking and nourishing. Each menu comes together in my head as I peruse the fresh produce at the market, the vibrant colors creating the kind of splendor that only nature can provide. It always makes me pause in wonder even on those days when I'm so busy I can barely stop to take a breath.

I have to say, though, that it's the action of the kitchen that drives my plant passion in ways that surprise me even after all these years. I never seem to tire of watching clear water sliding, glistening over the vegetables I am about to prepare, or the feel of my knife in my hand as I slice and dice my way through the ingredients. The perfumes of simmering stews and bubbling casseroles create the fragrances of a meal in progress.

You've heard all of this before. Chefs love to talk about food and the sheer joy it brings to them. We think of them as a special breed, delighted by every garlic clove they crush, every dish they garnish. But what about the rest of us? We're just trying to survive, right? Here's the thing. From setting the table (rather than eating over the sink out of a plastic takeaway container) to cleaning up, the passion for wellness is found in the simplest tasks if you let yourself go with it. When you pay attention to what you

cook, and how you cook, serve, and clean up afterward, you discover balance. You slow down just a little bit, enough to see the beauty of the world around you.

Think about meals around the table with people you love. Don't look now, but you're smiling at the thought. Those times connect us as one human family. Community, social justice, communication, sharing, and love are all learned at the table. Do it. Set the table and serve dinner, even if it's just you enjoying the meal. You'll discover a new kind of passion . . . for life and nourishment.

For me, cooking is a complete experience, not a chore to be endured at the end of a hectic day. I am convinced, down to the very core of my being, that if we are to create the life we want, we must begin to see food and cooking in a new light. We must remember that the act of cooking is the act of nourishing ourselves, so to say that we hate to cook—or we don't have time to cook—is to deny that we are of any value to ourselves or anyone else. Think about the impact of that statement.

Have I had to rethink my priorities to create the space in my day to cook meals? You bet I have. Have I seen the fruits of that reorganization? You bet I have. I face daily challenges just like everyone else. I have bad days and cranky days and low days just like everyone else. I get overwhelmed just like everyone else; I run two small businesses and a household. But through the preparation of daily meals and the ever-continuing observation of how food affects us, I have created a good life. I work very hard—and have the strength for that work. I face business stress every day—and I handle it with grace and balance (most of the time, anyway). And I can let go of it when it's done. The way I choose to eat has opened many doors for me, and not only in maintaining my health. It gives me the clarity of mind to see my way through any situation, making decisions and taking responsibility for the outcome.

I think that understanding the energy of food and how that energy behaves in our bodies, creating the people that we are, has given me freedom to follow the passions of my life. Being responsible can be seen as a burdensome load, as guilt and blame, or we can view responsibility as it is defined—as the ability to respond. Isn't that a liberating thought? Just think about it: the food we choose to eat can either enslave us or serve us as we strive to achieve our dreams. We get caught up in the day-to-day routine of survival in a world that seems to move faster and faster, threatening to leave us behind, or worse. It's time to care for ourselves, so that we have the strength to step back on the roller coaster of life each day, so that we remain an oasis of calm in the maelstrom of daily challenges.

That's what my work is about. I don't want to create another plan or system to achieve the perfect body, shiny hair, perfect health, and eternal youth. Lots of books promise us the moon, implying that we can have a problem-free life if only we read one more book or follow one more plan. Each time something "new" is marketed to you, you can rest assured that you'll be left ever so slightly disappointed, so you'll move on to the next trend. Ads tell us that if we just buy this one last dress, car, perfume, phone, tablet, computer, house, or patio set, we will feel complete. And yet, we never quite do, do we? Completion is designed to be just out of reach so we'll continue to consume.

That can be a real plus when it comes to life goals; we want to continue to reach for the stars. But with diet, food, consumerism, and wellness, not so much.

All the smoke and mirrors marketed to us have caused us to forget our essential nature, and those are the key ingredients to health and happiness. Once we understand who and what we are, it's an easy leap to knowing that what we eat creates the people we become.

I have learned there is no perfect life, no perfect health, no problem-free existence. The challenges of life make us stronger. And as humans, we are a part of nature. We can either fit in, contributing to the harmony of the planet, or we can go against natural law, creating disharmony in our environment and *dis-ease* for ourselves. Look what's happening to our precious planet right now as a result of our activities and carelessness (among other things).

Drawing from the ancient wisdom that is the foundation of every culture, I hope to give you tools to nourish yourself, your friends, and your family in a deliciously healthy way. I hope that you take away a better understanding of who you are, why you do what you do, why you feel as you do, and how the food you choose can help you achieve your dreams. I hope that you glean from my writing how profoundly food affects our bodies, minds, and spirits; how it can ignite your passions as it does mine. I hope that you are freed by this ancient thinking from all the dietary constraints that enslave you . . . from energy bars, smoothies, diet plans, calorie counting, and portion measuring. I hope you are freed to eat with abandon in a way that nourishes your body, mind, and spirit.

YOU AND YOUR CUTTING BOARD

My first cutting board is a family heirloom. You read that correctly . . . a family heirloom. My grandfather, my Pop, was a master carpenter and made a gorgeous cutting board for my grandmother that was the size of a small landing strip. She used it for everything, and by the time it was handed on to me, the center of the board was gently sloped from countless loaves of bread kneaded tenderly on its weathered surface.

I use my precious cutting board to this day for kneading bread and making pasta. While I have a new and totally gorgeous board for day-to-day use (the little slope in the center of my Nonna's board makes efficient chopping just impossible), I feel most connected to who I am when I have my family board on the counter and in use. I feel connected to my ancestry, my heritage, and my roots. It got me to thinking. Next to my chef's knife, my cutting board is my most important and revered kitchen tool. And that's as it should be.

While we're fascinated by cooking and food—watching cooking shows, buying books, and flocking to food festivals—getting us back to the kitchen and back to daily cooking has proven a bit more challenging. Sure, there are the various services that will deliver premeasured, prechopped foods with a recipe that you can assemble and cook, and I appreciate that effort. Anything to get you back to the kitchen.

However, those recipe and food delivery services leave me . . . cold, for lack of a better word. I have tried a few so that I could speak about them from experience. The food we "prepared" was delicious, to be sure, but we felt disconnected from it, as though someone else had prepared the meal for us. It felt false and foreign. It felt like eating out, but at home. I thought about it and decided it was because we weren't involved in the whole process. In order to take control of our wellness, we need to get back to the cutting board and prepare our food from scratch. Now before you slam the book shut and order takeout, let me explain.

Your cutting board is you. When you work on it regularly, it takes on the flavors of your kitchen, of how you cook. It becomes the old friend who knows you better than anyone: Sounds corny, right, this ode to a cutting board? Think of it this way: as your cutting board goes, so does your cooking. Is your board a teeny tiny cheese board that came with a fruit basket you received as a gift, tossed in a drawer, nicked and dusty? Is it flimsy plastic? Stained, cracked, or warped? Or is your board a wooden behemoth that takes up a good chunk of your counter space (that would be mine)?

Not all of us can buy artisanal handmade boards, but we can get our hands on a thick wooden board from a

kitchen shop. One of my cutting boards was made from a stair tread, stripped, smoothed, and naturally finished by a student at a local high school. There are bamboo boards and boards with little rubber feet for traction. Your budget (and workspace) will drive your decision, but try to go for the board that will give you enough space to work comfortably and is thick to prevent warping. Your cutting board says a lot about how you cook . . . or don't cook. In my kitchen, my old friend sits proudly on the counter all the time, ever at the ready for any task I might bring to her (yes, my cutting board is female). Clean and beautiful, sleek and deeply grounded to the Earth, my cutting board gives me confidence in the kitchen. She's part of the flavor of what I cook.

Getting back to the basics of cooking as you walk your path to wellness begins at the cutting board. As you slice and dice vegetables for various luscious dishes, it's your chef's knife and cutting board that will become your most intimate and proactive partners. They'll work with you to flavor your dishes, to enhance your experience of cooking. They're the foundation of delivering your plant-passionate message of love, health, and nourishment from the stove to the table.

My cutting board is the anchor of my kitchen, anticipating the first knife stroke of the day. I love her as I love a girlfriend, and sometimes I think she knows me better than I know myself.

This may sound like a lot of power to give that piece of wood that allows you to slice and dice, but when I think of going back to basics—of cooking to create health and wellness, of nourishing our bodies as best we can—I can't think of that process without paying homage to my dear friend, my cutting board.

CHAPTER 1

BACK TO THE CUTTING BOARD

The simple act of cooking has taken on meaning that we can barely fathom anymore. Is it a coliseum-type sporting event with chefs running around a kitchen cooking sea urchin and circus peanuts? Is it a Nonna-like chef taking us back with recipes nostalgic for our youth?

The art of cooking now comes complete with an anxiety driven by celebrity, information overload, and pressure to continuously channel your inner Julia Child and nutritionist at the same time. We must impress! We must stress over every bite, every swoosh of sauce, every carbohydrate or gram of protein or sugar. It's no wonder that so few of us are comfortable in the kitchen these days. I'm here to ask you to set all that tension and pretense aside and rediscover your passion for the art of cooking.

Cookbooks inspire me, especially those written for people who say they can't cook or simply don't have the time. They focus on the basics of cooking with variations to allow for success for anyone, whether a complete novice or the most seasoned cook. I repeatedly fall in love with the idea of freeing people from the stress that can be characteristic of healthy cooking. This thinking is what inspired me to write about life in the kitchen from the perspective of making the healthiest choices you can for your family and for you.

MY RULES OF THE KITCHEN

Using the freshest ingredients available to you turns cooking into the easiest (and most pleasurable) passionate pastime in the world. Fresh foods need little enhancement to be their most luscious. Great olive oil, fresh lemon juice, and sea salt are the ingredients I use most frequently to bring the best out in any dish, along with a little parsley and maybe some garlic. Besides that, there are some nuggets of wisdom that I would love to share with you after a lifetime (nearly . . . I've been cooking since I was a child) of cooking and creating recipes.

To Taste or Not to Taste

Many chefs and cooks like to taste and taste often. If that works for you, then taste and do it often. If you don't cook now, I'd advise you to make this a practice until you know what a dish should taste like, or how you would like a dish to taste. After that, you have options. When my mother was teaching me to cook, she would stop me, saying, "Use all your senses. There's more to cooking than tasting the food. Anyone can do that." She taught me to see the food, feel the food (not literally, but with my intuition), smell the food, and listen to the food. Taste as you learn the essentials of seasoning, then make it a goal to taste less and *feel* more.

Fresh Stuff

My mother used to say that the best meals came from the freshest ingredients. She was right. My advice to you as you venture into cooking is to buy fresh ingredients. You don't need to break the bank. Just about every shop, bodega, market, big box store, and warehouse club has fresh produce that you can use in your cooking. If you can't find fresh, grab some frozen veggies, as they are most often frozen at the peak of their freshness. I'm not a fan of canned vegetables because they are limp, tasteless, and not rich in nutrition. But if canned vegetables are your only option, then use them. Just use vegetables in your cooking. No excuses.

Get Yourself a Timer

Seriously, get a timer. I use mine all the time for all sorts of dishes, from beans to soups to grains and desserts. I use it so that I don't forget something on the stove if I am cooking a large meal and get lost in another task (which I do . . . a lot). I time every dessert so I don't over- or under-bake. I time beans so they are cooked to their perfect tenderness and are not hard or mushy. A timer frees you to multitask and not lose track.

Use Leftovers Wisely

Simply eating leftovers out of a container might be easy, but man, it can be boring. And that's the good news. Eating the same food, day after day, reheated or simply brought to room temperature, is not only uninspiring, but it can also cause you to feel lethargic, crave sweets, and feel less in love with the food you cook. Leftovers can be crazy valuable to us in the kitchen, but they're best when they're repurposed somehow in new and yummy dishes. Try using leftover bean stews to create soups or spreads to slather on bread, or add leftover cooked greens to a fresh salad in another meal. Cooked whole grains can be added to soups, turned into salads, or stir-fried with veggies for a quick and nutritious meal. It's lovely to cook every dish fresh from scratch, but living in the real world often prevents that luxury. Planning ahead to use leftovers in combination with fresh ingredients will help you pull together simple dishes that create balance and reduce the stress of meal prep.

Use Your Knife Well

One of the biggest challenges many cooks face is using a knife well and to your best advantage. While you see impressive arrays of knives on most chefs' worktables, many of us will confess that we mostly use our aptly named chef's knife. I love knives and have a host of them, but I always turn to my favorite chef's knife when it's time to cook. While this knife is my go-to tool, I will occasionally use a paring knife to take stems out of strawberries or peel a cucumber or potato, and I always slice bread with a serrated knife to avoid dulling the blade of my chef's knife. Get one that you love. Hold a variety of them in your hand before you decide on this most important tool. You'll know the right one when you feel it. Trust me.

Seasoning

This one is subjective, as people like different flavors in their food. It's also a bit of an art form, finding the right nuance of flavor you like, so experiment and cook . . . a lot. Food should taste like itself, but enhanced, like its best self, not like salt, pepper, hot spice, or herbs and spices. They are all simply ways to bring out the natural flavors of foods; you don't want a hostile takeover of your dish.

I usually salt near the end of cooking so that my food has time to become tender and the salt blends into the ingredients, with just a pinch at the beginning to coax the natural flavors forth. While I may use pinches of salt as I sauté, I season fully around 7 minutes before I call a dish done. This helps me avoid adding salt at the table, which can result in a dish being too salty. Spices and dried herbs are added to my dishes at the beginning of cooking, while fresh herbs are added at the end, right before serving. I rarely use dried herbs and prefer the flavor of fresh, with the exception of oregano (it has more intense flavor dried than fresh). To maintain freshness, I buy spices and dried herbs in small quantities—they can lose their flavor if kept for too long.

MY PLANT-PASSIONATE PANTRY

As you cook and your passion grows, you will want to flesh out your pantry, choosing a variety of ingredients that reflect the cooking culture of your kitchen. You may even want to venture into the world of natural baking, which will create the need for other ingredients, so I have created a separate list of baking essentials. As you read these lists, don't get crazy. Stock your pantry bit by bit; your cooking style and ingredients should reflect your tastes.

WHOLE GRAINS
Short- and medium-grain
  brown rice
Quinoa
Millet
Corn (organic)
Whole oat groats
Kasha (buckwheat)
Barley
Farro
Spelt

CRACKED GRAINS
Rolled and steel-cut oats
Corn grits
Couscous
Bulgur

BEANS
Lentils
Black beans
Chickpeas
White beans

CONDIMENTS
Extra-virgin olive oil
Avocado oil
Sunflower oil (non-GMO)
Light sesame oil
Brown rice vinegar
Red wine vinegar
Umeboshi vinegar
Balsamic vinegar
Sea salt
Black pepper
Dried herbs and spices
  of your choice

DRIED FOODS
Dried daikon
Dried shiitake mushrooms
Dried maitake mushrooms
Sea vegetables:
  Nori
  Wakame
  Kombu
  Arame
  Hiziki
Nuts and seeds
Kuzu and/or arrowroot
  powder (used for
  thickening, like
  cornstarch)

OTHER
Whole-grain bread
Dried pasta
Fruit preserves

IN THE FRIDGE
Leafy greens
Kale
Collards
Watercress
Bok choy
Mustard greens
Escarole
Broccoli Rabe
Arugula
Lettuce
Parsley
Scallions

GROUND, ROUND, AND ROOT VEGETABLES
Cabbage
Chinese cabbage
Cauliflower
Broccoli
Brussels sprouts
Turnip
Parsnip
Daikon
Radish
Burdock
Lotus root
Carrot
Rutabaga
Tomatoes (in season)
Zucchini (in season)
Onion

FERMENTED FOODS
Miso
Sauerkraut
Soy sauce and tamari
Fresh unpasteurized pickles

FRUIT
Seasonal fresh fruit

BAKING INGREDIENTS
Whole wheat pastry flour
Sprouted wheat flour
Baking powder (aluminum-free)
Baking soda
Pure vanilla extract
Coconut sugar
Brown rice syrup
Vegan butter substitute

You'll add ingredients like dark chocolate, dried fruit, and nuts as you develop your dessert skills and repertoire.

YOUR TOOLS

A well-equipped kitchen will help you work easily and efficiently. I keep the utensils and tools I use often right near my work space in pretty clay pitchers, so I am not hunting for things as I cook. It adds beauty to my counter and makes me want to be in the kitchen by seducing me into a gorgeous environment.

That said, I hate gadgets. I'm glad that's off my chest. From garlic presses to citrus juicers, I have little use for any of them.* Give me a chef's knife, wooden spoons, and a cutting board and I'm all set. Every time I see a cute new doodad (that's all I can think to call them), what comes to mind is that it's another thing to clean. But that's me. If you love gadgets and simply must have the latest, greatest tool to make life easier, go for it. But if you're like me, you want to streamline, reduce consumption, and control how much stuff clutters your life . . . and your kitchen. In that vein of simple living and simple cooking, I've compiled a list of tools designed to make life easier in the kitchen.

ESSENTIAL TOOLS TO COOK ANYTHING

Knives

A kitchen without a great chef's knife is nonfunctioning. You don't need to spend a fortune, but you need to head to a kitchen shop where you can hold the knife and see if you like the heft and balance. I advise between 7 and 8 inches for the blade length. While I prefer a ceramic knife, a solid stainless steel blade that costs under $50 will serve you just fine. You can grow your knife collection as you grow your skills, but I suspect you will fall in love with one knife and remain monogamous.

Cutting Board

The second most important tool in the kitchen, a thick wooden board will change how you cook. Thick boards won't crack or warp and will last a long time. Get a board that suits your space and budget, but as big as your space allows so you have room to work. I like a thick board on rubber feet so water doesn't accumulate underneath and the little feet hold it in place. Bamboo is also a great choice, as it's light and naturally antibacterial. Don't even think about those flimsy roll-up plastic ones . . . just don't.

---

* *All this posturing about gadgets and consumption aside, I must be truthful. As an avid baker, I am in the midst of a long, passionate affair with my stand mixer that shows no signs of abating. I often say I couldn't live without her. She is my one gadget weakness.*

10-Inch Cast-Iron or Stainless Steel Skillet

I want to say you need both of these in your kitchen and I might even add a "green" nonstick skillet as well. Most people struggle with seasoning a cast-iron pan (to avoid rust), so stainless steel is a good choice for everyday cooking. It distributes heat evenly and cleans easily. Should you decide that you want to cook with cast iron, here's how to season: sauté an onion in a generous amount of inexpensive oil and salt. Discard the onion, oil, and salt, wipe the skillet, and repeat this process twice more. Wipe the skillet very well, including the bottom and the handle, then cure it in the oven for 1 hour at 275°F. Cast iron is worth the effort.

Sieve and/or Colander

A sieve and/or colander comes in handy for rinsing grains and beans, draining pasta, and lifting boiled or blanched vegetables from boiling water. I use mine every day and prefer a fine sieve over a colander because I use it the way most people use a slotted spoon.

Saucepans (2- to 3-Quart)

The number of people you're regularly cooking for will determine the size of this pan, but every kitchen needs a small saucepan (or two or three) for steaming, boiling, blanching, and making sauces and small pots of soup. I have several smaller pans, as I cook for two people most nights.

Dutch Oven

There's no chili, stew, pasta, or boiled vegetables without a large Dutch oven. The average size is 5 to 6 quarts, and it will serve you in cooking for one or for a crowd. If you're boiling pasta, stainless steel is a good choice. If you make lots of soups and stews, or stove top–to-oven braises and casseroles, consider adding a porcelain-coated cast-iron pot, such as those made by Le Creuset.

Tongs

A good set of long-handled tongs does a lot of jobs, from mixing salads to lifting foods from boiling water to turning foods on the grill. I like metal or wooden tongs for salads and tossing ingredients and tongs with silicone tips that can stand heat in pans or on grills.

Wooden Spoons

Wooden spoons add a beauty and grace to cooking that I love. They're easy on your hands for holding; they don't scrape the pans' surfaces; they clean easily; and they don't make irritating noise in the kitchen (a big one for me). I have many, all made from sustainable cherry wood, but a few will get you started. Go with a 10-inch, a 12-inch, and a 14-inch to serve you best in just about any task.

I'm not a fan of silicone spatulas, brushes, and metal spoons. I have a couple, but I just don't consider them essential.

Measuring Spoons and Cups

I have to confess: I rarely measure or use measuring spoons or cups unless I'm testing a recipe for a new cookie or cake. But for most of us, measuring is key to the success of recipes, so get a set of measuring cups and spoons. I like stainless steel measuring tools, as they last and last and clean easily.

Microplane or Box Grater

I use my microplane so often, I feel like it's an extension of my arm! From zesting citrus to grating nutmeg, a microplane is easy to handle and gives you a finely grated texture. A box grater is very different, doing different work, like coarse grating for fritters, salads, or cakes. I don't use one as often as I use my microplane, but it's a solid tool to have in your kitchen for easy prep with certain dishes.

Baking Equipment

You'll need baking sheets, rimmed and without rims. You'll need an 8 x 8-inch baking pan, a 9 x 13-inch baking pan, a wire cooling rack, muffin tins and papers, and any other baking tool that makes your heart beat a little faster. You may also wish to add a scale if you find that you're baking often and want to measure accurately every time.

BECOME A MASTER OF TECHNIQUE

There are basic cooking techniques to master that will serve you well and make you the plant-passionate cook you long to be. Once you have them in your repertoire, you can combine them to create incredible dishes, like sautéing veggies before turning them into a soup, stew, or casserole.

Mastering blanching, boiling, roasting, braising, sautéing, stir-frying, stewing, and pickling will have you cooking up a storm, and no one has to know how easy it all is. In vegetable cooking, the biggest challenge lies in the preparation of the veggies—the slicing and dicing. Developing your knife skills is paramount to being efficient in cooking and, sadly, there's no shortcut in this process. Only practice will streamline how you function in your kitchen space. You must pick up your knife regularly for it to become an extension of who you are and how you cook. Cooking techniques are simple, straightforward, and easily mastered. It's usually the chopping that discourages people.

But I'm here to tell you that once you master the basic skills, there's no feast too big or snack too small for you to conquer. Not mastering these skills will leave you chronically flustered and at odds with creating meals. But remember what I said earlier. I am a lazy cook at heart and take no steps in cooking that I don't need to take, so these skills I am asking you to master will create a foundation for your cooking to soar.

AT THE CUTTING BOARD

Now that you have a great knife, you'll need to learn how to slice and dice ingredients to bring out their best qualities. How do we know how big or small, chunky or fine, to cut veggies for various dishes? Do we *really* need to peel our vegetables? These simple guidelines will get you started.

For soups, you can never dice veggies too small. The tinier, the better; this helps the soup become sweet, as the sugars from the veggies "bleed" into the broth. For stews and casseroles, hearty chunks of veggies will stand up to long cooking times without losing texture and turning to mush. Fine julienne and shredding are the perfect cuts for salads, blanching, and quick stir-fry dishes where you want the veggies to cook quickly but maintain some crunch.

I am not a peeler. It's the rare occasion that I take the outer skin off a veggie, even with nonorganic items. You can't peel the pesticides off, and why lose those surface nutrients and fiber? The exception is obviously waxed vegetables. That can lead to an awful aftertaste in the food you cook, so peel those, please.

Before chopping, wash the vegetable and wet your cutting board with a sponge or a wet cloth. Wetting the board prevents the wood from absorbing nutrients and moisture. Chopping on a dry board results in drier, less tasty ingredients.

Practice various knife cuts until you're efficient. You won't develop skills if you don't practice. Will you be slow and clumsy at first? Yup. Will you develop some fine skills with practice? Yup. It's veggie chopping, not brain surgery.

When it comes to vegetable prep, it's important to breathe. Relax and enjoy the process of cooking. It's sexy and fun if you allow yourself to be in the space. I know we are all busy and often preparing food under less than ideal circumstances, between soccer games, with screaming kids and frazzled spouses running around, or after a long day. But if you can breathe into it, and lean into the process of slicing and dicing, you'll find yourself relaxed and happy.

It's not a race. Your goal is to create cuts that are the same size and thickness, for a dish that is flavorful, attractive, and evenly cooked. Speed will come as you gain experience and confidence.

DICING

For round vegetables, cut them in half lengthwise and lay each half on its flat side on the board. This makes it less likely that you will cut yourself, as the vegetable can't roll around. Slice the vegetable lengthwise into slices that are as thick as the size of the dice you want—for instance, for a ¼-inch dice (which is the size you're going for when the recipe says to "dice"), slice the vegetable into ¼-inch slices. Stack the slices and cut into spears. Gather the spears and cut crosswise to create a dice. This method works for any round veggie, from turnips to cabbage to onions to beets.

For long vegetables, like cucumber, carrot, and parsnip, trim the tips as needed. Slice the vegetable in half lengthwise and lay each half on its flat side on the board. Cut each half into long spears; again, the thickness of the spears dictates the size of the dice. Gather the spears and cut crosswise to create a dice.

Mincing is simply very small dicing, made by cutting the vegetables into slender matchsticks and then cutting across.

STEP 1

STEP 2

STEP 3

STEP 4

JULIENNE/MATCHSTICK

Trim the tips off the vegetable (such as a carrot) that you are planning to julienne. Lay the vegetable on the cutting board, on an angle, holding the thicker end. Slice the veggie into thin diagonal pieces. If your knife is sharp, the slices will fall onto themselves, resembling fallen dominoes. You may need to rearrange the slices slightly to achieve this effect as you practice. Once the vegetable is sliced, hold the overlapped pieces in place with your hand, spreading your fingers to hold as many of the pieces in place as possible. Cut lengthwise across the pieces to create long, slender matchstick pieces.

For round vegetables, simply cut in half lengthwise and lay each half on its flat side on the board. Thinly slice lengthwise; stack the slices and slice into thin julienne spears.

STEP 1   STEP 2

SHREDDING

To shred veggies such as cabbage, you have two choices. Pull off a few outer leaves, roll them into cylinders, and thinly slice crosswise to create long threads. You may also cut the vegetable in half and lay the flat side on the board and slice crosswise into threads. This is more challenging because the cabbage can be large and unwieldy to hold.

For leafy greens, simply trim off the tips of the stems. Leave the stems intact. They are loaded with valuable minerals, as their purpose is to draw nutrients from the soil into the leaves. Roll the leaves into cylinders and slice them crosswise into threads. If the stems are very thick, simply fold each leaf in half, exposing the stem. Slice the stem out of the green, then slice it and cook it separately. After removing the stem, roll and cut the leaves as directed above.

STEP 1

STEP 2

STEP 3

CHUNK OR ROLL CUT

To cut round vegetables into chunks for stewing, roasting, or braising, cut the vegetable in half lengthwise and lay the flat side on the board. Cut it into thick wedges, then gather the wedges and cut crosswise to create the size chunk you want.

For long vegetables, trim the ends and lay the vegetable on the board, holding onto the thicker end. With your knife at an angle, cut crosswise, taking a chunk off the end. Roll the vegetable 90 degrees and cut again. Keep rolling and cutting until you have cut the entire vegetable, adjusting the degree of rolling so that the pieces are similar in size when you are through.

STEP 1

STEP 2

STEP 3

STEP 4

THE YIN/YANG FACTOR

When I recovered my health with cooking, I made a life-changing discovery: there's more to food than food. I try to be up front with people, so I will tell you right now that this thinking is a bit esoteric—you may find it a little "out there" at first. When I first studied this philosophy, I thought it was a different language and, in a way, it is. It rocked my world and once I began to understand this ancient wisdom, I felt as though a veil had been lifted and I could see clearly the essential nature of *nature itself*.

It's my hope for you that this introduction to this ancient way of looking at nature helps you understand the what, how, and why of cooking and eating naturally in our modern world. I hope that it empowers you to make choices based on the purpose of your life and that it enables you to become a proactive participant in creating wellness.

THE FORCES OF LIFE

The universe in which we live is an endless interplay of opposing natural forces, flowing from physical matter to energy to physical matter to energy in a continuing cycle of construction and destruction, and of expansion and contraction. The basic theories of physics were founded on this thinking. The interaction of the two essential forces, called yin and yang by the Chinese, create an unending pattern of action that creates all the phenomena we see and experience in nature. Yin is symbolic of energy that is primarily expansive and outward in its movement, going from the physical to the nonphysical. Yang, on the other hand, is symbolic of energy that is primarily contracting or constricting and inward in its movement, constructing the physical. These energies, while opposite, aren't distinct or separate from each other; they come together to form one energetic interaction, constantly changing from one to the other and back, expanding and contracting. This interaction of opposites is what makes nature come alive.

This is the pulse of life as we know it. Think about it. Your lungs expand and contract as you breathe; your intestines expand and contract as nourishment is extracted from food; youth changes to age; fall becomes spring and back again in an endless cycle of death and rebirth.

The basic concepts of yin and yang form the foundation for much of Eastern philosophy and, as a result, many natural modalities used in healing and wellness. Here is the thinking: all of nature is part of one; no one phenomenon is independent of any other. All things are dependent on each other's function and existence, and this interdependence forms one continuing pattern of action.

A basic tenet of this philosophy is that everything changes, meaning that all of nature is in a constant state of motion. Nothing is static; a state of flux is the norm, even if we can't see or feel it. Both expansion and contraction exist in all things, complementing each other as they interact: opening and closing, appearing and disintegrating.

In this dance of life, in all phenomena, both yin and yang are present, with one or the other as the dominant energy. Each plant, animal, person, fish, bug, or any other living thing, food, or phenomenon will either appear contracted or more relaxed in its overall natural character, while its opposite nature may be minimal or even dormant. Rocks appear hard, and water soft, but rocks can be ground into powder and water frozen into ice.

The idea that all physical matter is made up of energy is one that is completely accepted in the scientific world of physics and other sciences, where esoteric thinking plays a very small role. Freed from the constraints of scientific thinking, Eastern philosophers seemed to shroud this simple theory in mysticism, making it hard to understand and untenable for many people. You might ask why. If this theory is reflective of the patterns of nature, what's so tough about that? Part of the issue is that these philosophers were deeply rooted in the rhythms of nature. Their lives depended on it. As modern people, ours do not.

It's hard to accept the world as energy because we have lost touch with the rhythms of nature. We live in increasingly artificial environments—in air-conditioned or overheated homes, in windowless offices, in cars. We can go for days without feeling the power of the Earth under our feet. The rhythms of energy feel foreign to us when we live our lives apart from nature and immersed in technology.

For our ancestors, understanding the environment in which they lived was the key to their survival. Knowing when the cold winds were coming, when the monsoon season would arrive, or when a drought was likely to occur was essential to a successful harvest or hunt. It meant the continuance of their cultures. While no longer vital to our physical survival, understanding nature is vital to our health and our ability to be responsible for ourselves and the health of our families, society, and, ultimately, our planet.

RECONNECTING WITH OUR NATURAL SELVES

When we use our perceptive abilities to explore our environment, we experience an expansive, more emotional, and spiritual awareness of our surroundings. This quality is characteristically yin, or expanded. When our physical senses allow us to take in our environment, to gather information and nutrition, this process of construction and maintenance is yang—contracted, increasing our physical control over our environment. Depending on our activity, location, and purpose, one of these energies will dominate the moment, so we get the most useful information for the situation and can act appropriately.

Wait, *what?* This can be confusing, so let's look at this example.

Digestion is a simple physical example of yin/yang in action. This bodily system is a series of hollow organs (yin) whose jobs are to absorb nutrients by breaking down the dense, physical (yang) food we take in. Our nervous system, on the other hand, is an organized, compact, complicated (yang) system that allows us to scope out our environment, to perceive energy and natural rhythms that surround us (yin). These two systems, while opposite, work hand in hand to nourish us on all levels—physical and sensual. Make sense?

As human beings, it's important to understand that all sensory information that we receive and how we process that information is key to the quality of our existence. What we see, hear, feel, touch, and smell has the potential to benefit or nourish us, or not. Truly healthy people feed themselves by assimilating lots of information, both physical and nonphysical. They continually seek "nourishment" by pursuing challenges, and by placing themselves in situations that create a deeper understanding of life. This adaptability and vitality that we think of only as curiosity creates a healthy mind and body. As we grow further away from nature, we lose our innate ability to connect with our natural environment. To return to our true human selves, we must reconnect to nature and understand the vital rhythms that govern us. Then we can be fully responsible and in control of how we feel and how we fit in the world.

OTHER STUFF YOU SHOULD KNOW ABOUT VEGETABLE PREP

Now that you are on your way to mastering knife skills, there are a few more tips before we get to the stove and begin cooking.

When you buy produce, don't wash it before putting it in the fridge. It will shorten the life of whatever you buy. And don't wrap your produce in paper towels in plastic bags—you'll dry out the produce and waste paper, hurting your vegetables and the environment.

Before you pop your produce in the fridge, remove any rubber bands or binders around bunches so air can circulate, then store with the bags loosely open. You will get about four to five days out of delicate vegetables like fresh basil, arugula, spinach, and parsley before the flavor begins to wane. Expect at least a week of freshness when storing kale, collard greens, bok choy, and broccoli. Hardier vegetables like cauliflower, cabbage, and most roots will last for at least two weeks or longer if refrigerated.

Foods like onions, tomatoes, winter squash, apples, pears, oranges, peaches, grapefruit, bananas, lemons, limes, and avocados should not be in the fridge. It compromises their flavors; they taste like cardboard. When left on the counter or windowsill, vegetables and fruits will have superior flavor, plus they look gorgeous and bring life to the room.

When you're cooking, you may not use the whole carrot, parsnip, squash, onion, or cabbage. Wrap unused pieces in the bag it came from (or plastic wrap) and return it to the fridge. Once cut, all produce must be refrigerated, including onions, or it will rot quickly. And when you split a winter squash, be sure to remove the seeds from both halves, even if you are not using the whole squash. Storing cut squash with the seeds inside will cause it to sour quickly. Remove the seeds and wrap the unused piece in a produce bag, and you will get at least ten days' life out of each squash.

Cut vegetables should be used within 24 to 48 hours, or they will spoil, and that's just wasteful.

AT THE STOVE

Cooking simply can be elegant and satisfying. You only need to master a few basic techniques to create a great meal, no matter what television chefs or molecular gastronomists tell you.

miso, takes about ten minutes to prepare and provides a flexible energy to start the day. Lightly cooked vegetables with whole-grain toast are another simple start. And if you need extra energy, an easily digested protein, like lightly cooked tofu, fits the bill perfectly, with its powerful energy and relaxed nature.

I reserve things like fruit, muffins, and breakfast pastries for very special occasions. These foods, while simple and surely the easy way out, really don't serve us all that well. When we get up in the morning, we've been fasting for several hours while we sleep. What we eat as our first food will set the mood for the balance of the day. If our first food is simple sugar, like fruit and fruit juice, sweet pastries, and muffins, we immediately alter our blood chemistry; we set ourselves up for a roller-coaster day, with our energy and moods rising and falling as dramatically as our blood sugar. We're better off with lightly cooked vegetables than fruit, as they'll keep us feeling fresh and relaxed, without the drama of sugar. Remember, there are no rules that say you can't eat vegetables before noon. It's a rare occasion that finds sweets as the breakfast food in our house.

And then there are special occasions—you know them—the relaxed Sunday brunches with friends where we hang around munching for hours. It's good to occasionally free yourself to enjoy everything, from whole-grain porridge and cooked veggies with miso soup, to cinnamon buns and breakfast breads, to sautéed veggies and tofu.

The bottom line? Give some thought and effort to this most important meal. It'll seem like you have more time and energy to achieve your daily goals with ease and grace. Wouldn't it be great to be rid of those mornings when you drag yourself out of bed and dread the day, and replace them with an outlook as bright as the sun outside your window?

WHAT'S FOR LUNCH?

Lunch is easy, whether you have the luxury of eating it at your own kitchen table, tote it to work with you, or regularly dine out with clients on business.

The easiest lunch I can advise for you—and the most substantial—is to cook a bit of extra food for dinner and simply pack your lunch from dinner leftovers. You're all set with a delicious and completely nourishing lunch. I highly recommend this option for people who are super active and need more calories.

You can take a thermos of homemade soup with a simple sandwich for a lighter meal. I like hummus on pita bread or baked tofu with lettuce on whole-grain bread. This lunch, which feels light, is anything but—the nutrient-dense ingredients provide stamina and energy to carry you through the afternoon.

Eating out at lunch is a snap now that plant-passionate eating has gone mainstream. Just about every restaurant has something vegan on offer, and while it won't be home cooked by you, that's just fine now and again. Just bear in mind that eating out, even at the grooviest vegan joint, will give you more fat, sugar, and salt than you might want to eat.

And finally, for a truly light lunch, try noodles in soup or a platter of lightly cooked vegetables with a dip, like hummus. Lunch can be as simple or as substantial as your body and lifestyle need it to be to sustain you.

DINNER IN

For some of us, dinner is the main meal of the day. We're finally home, ready to chill for the evening, so we make a meal that's more substantial. We sit around the table and catch up on each other's day. For others, dinner is on the run, going from work to soccer practice, the gym, or some other social obligation, which makes sitting around the table a rare treat reserved for holidays or weekends.

In any event, dinner is the last full meal of your day and a time to examine what your body still needs to feel nourished. In our house, if we have a substantial breakfast and lunch, then dinner is as simple as soup and a salad to end the day because we tend to eat later in the evening after long days. On the weekends, when we have more leisure time, dinner will be a feast of whole grains, beans, veggies, and soups served in multiple courses at a relaxed pace.

Planning dinner takes a bit of thinking ahead. If I know I'll be walking in the door from the gym at 7 p.m., hungry and a little tired, I'll plan to cook a bit extra at another meal so I can quickly combine the leftovers with fresh vegetables to create a soup or stew that will serve as our main (and only) course, with a crisp salad on the side. For instance, if I'm making a lentil soup or stew, I'll cook some extra lentils to use in another dish within the next couple of days. When grains are on the menu, I cook more rice or quinoa than I know we will eat, so that I have the base for a salad or stir-fry on another night.

less for food. And then there are the lovely sea plants that provide us with incredible amounts of vitamins and minerals and comprise a small part of our nutrition.

Did you know that the word "vegetable" comes from the Latin verb *vegere*, which means "to animate or enliven"? Flowering plants, which provide the bulk of our nutrition, are the most highly developed of the seed plants. This group of plant life contains more varieties than all the other groups combined, and seed plants comprise the great majority of the vegetables we eat. Many of these vegetables can be consumed in their entirety, while we utilize only parts of others, depending on the energy and nutrients we want and need at any given time.

We eat vegetables at every meal in our house. I know, I know. Eating vegetables for breakfast sounds odd. But is it? Think hash browns or Western omelets, avocado toast or green juice. Is it *really* that left of center to eat vegetables for breakfast? I find it refreshing and comforting, to be honest.

As with all our meals, fresh vegetables are best when cooked simply. For the first meal of the day, I boil them in lightly salted water until bright in color and crisp-tender and serve them with a squirt of fresh lemon juice, or season them with salt or soy sauce and stew them until deliciously soft. At other meals, simple boiled vegetables are served with a drizzle of great olive oil and that same squirt of lemon juice. You're thinking that it sounds plain, right? But when veggies are fresh and seasonal, uncomplicated cooking enhances their character and allows them to shine.

I cook simply overall (are you sensing a theme here?), but I love to incorporate sautés, stews, and braising in my vegetable preparation. Meals in our house are decidedly plant-centric, so it's not uncommon for us to have a soup with two vegetable dishes and a fresh salad to make our dinner. That may sound overwhelming, but most dishes take just moments to prepare and cooking time involves almost no work at all.

Let's cook some veggies, okay?

CANDIED PARSNIP AND CARROT TATIN

This pretty cake is a splendid sweet and savory side dish. Smothered in caramelized, sweet root vegetables and topped with an orange-scented glaze, it brings together the most delicious complementary flavors.

Makes 6 to 8 servings

SAVORY CAKE

2½ cups whole wheat pastry or sprouted whole wheat flour
2 teaspoons baking powder
2 teaspoons sesame seeds
1 teaspoon baking soda
1 teaspoon dried basil
1 teaspoon dried rosemary, crushed
Generous pinch sea salt
¼ cup avocado or extra-virgin olive oil
½ to 1 cup unsweetened almond, oat, or soy milk

TOPPING

2 teaspoons avocado or extra-virgin olive oil
4 carrots, halved lengthwise
4 parsnips, halved lengthwise
Organic soy sauce, to taste
4 tablespoons brown rice syrup
Grated zest and juice of 1 orange

To make the cake: Preheat the oven to 350°F. In a medium bowl, combine the flour, baking powder, sesame seeds, baking soda, basil, rosemary, and sea salt and mix well. Set aside.

Begin the topping: Heat the oil in a 10-inch ovenproof skillet (I like cast iron for this recipe) over medium-high heat. Stir in the carrot and parsnip halves, season lightly with the soy sauce, and stir until shiny with oil. Arrange the vegetables in a decorative pattern, covering the bottom of the pan. Add the brown rice syrup and orange zest and reduce the heat to medium. Cook until the glaze is thick and syrupy and the veggies are golden brown, 8 to 10 minutes, stirring occasionally so you can feel the glaze thicken. Remove from the heat and stir in the orange juice.

Mix the oil into the dry cake ingredients, then slowly stir in the milk until a smooth, spoonable batter forms. Spoon the batter evenly over the cooked vegetables, taking care not to disturb your pattern. Bake for 35 to 40 minutes, until the center of the cake springs back to the touch. Cool the cake for about 10 minutes, then run a sharp knife around the rim of the skillet to loosen the cake. Place your serving platter over the skillet and carefully invert the cake. If any of the vegetables stick to the pan, simply remove them and replace them on the cake top. Serve warm or hot.

SWEET ROOT VEGETABLE STEW

There's nothing quite like sweet root vegetables to create calm strength. In cooler weather, this splendid side dish will keep you toasty warm by igniting your digestive Fire, but that doesn't mean you can't enjoy this in warm weather, too. Just cut the vegetables in smaller pieces, cook for a shorter time, and get your strength without building up internal heat. You can also vary the vegetables as the seasons and your tastes dictate.

Makes 3 to 4 servings

1 (1-inch) piece kombu or 1 bay leaf

1 sweet onion, cut into thick wedges

1 large carrot, large roll-cut pieces

1 large parsnip, large roll-cut pieces

1 small daikon, large roll-cut pieces

2 cups (1-inch) winter squash cubes, such as butternut, kabocha, hokkaido, or acorn

Grated zest of 1 lemon

3 to 4 tablespoons unfiltered apple juice

2 tablespoons mirin or white wine

Organic soy sauce, to taste

Place the kombu or bay leaf in a heavy pot. Layer the onion, carrot, parsnip, and daikon, followed by the winter squash. Top with the lemon zest, then add enough apple juice to just cover the bottom of the pan. Sprinkle lightly with the mirin (or wine) and soy sauce. Cover and bring to a low boil over medium-low heat, watching the heat to avoid a heavy boil.

When the stew reaches a gentle boil, cover, reduce the heat to low, and simmer until the vegetables are tender but not mushy, 30 to 35 minutes. Season lightly with a little more soy sauce and simmer, uncovered, until any remaining liquid has been absorbed into the stew and the apple juice and mirin have reduced to a slightly sticky glaze. Remove and discard the kombu (or bay leaf) and serve immediately.

COOK'S TIP: *Organic soy sauce provides that mysterious flavor we know as "umami." It's richer than simple sea salt and provides a depth of flavor that is unparalleled in certain dishes. I use it often, but not always, because you don't want all your recipes to taste like a stir-fry. Use it lightly as you would any salt. It's designed to enhance food, not overpower it, so my guiding principle is to add ½ teaspoon to a dish designed for four people and adjust up from there. You can always make a dish more flavorful, but if you add too much soy sauce, like salt, you will ruin the dish.*

CANDIED SWEET POTATOES AND PARSNIPS WITH BITTER GREENS

The intense sweetness of this side dish will make you feel relaxed. The root vegetables keep your feet on the ground and the bitter greens provide flexibility, clarity of mind, and strong red blood cells. I love to use garnet sweet potatoes in this recipe for their bright, jewel-like color and sweet flavor.

Makes 3 to 4 servings

2 parsnips, cut into 2-inch roll-cut chunks

1 sweet potato, cut into 2-inch roll-cut chunks

2 tablespoons extra-virgin olive oil

2 teaspoons sea salt

1 tablespoon balsamic vinegar

1 tablespoon brown rice syrup

Grated zest of 1 lemon

1 bunch bitter greens, such as escarole or watercress, rinsed well

Preheat the oven to 375°F.

Place the parsnips and sweet potato in a large mixing bowl. Drizzle in the olive oil, season with salt, and toss to coat.

Transfer the vegetables to a shallow baking dish, avoiding overlap. Drizzle the balsamic vinegar and rice syrup over the vegetables, then sprinkle the lemon zest over the dish. Cover and bake for 35 minutes. Uncover and return to the oven to tenderize the veggies and brown the edges, another 7 to 10 minutes.

While the vegetables bake, tear the greens into small pieces using your hands. To serve, gently stir the fresh greens into the cooked veggies. Serve hot.

BURDOCK KINPIRA

In the traditional version of this dish, intensely strengthening burdock and gently strengthening carrot are cooked as a high fire sauté for energy, then simmered for quiet endurance. This version, a powerhouse of energy in its own right, has a few more ingredients and is simply sautéed, giving high energy and enduring stamina.

Makes 3 to 4 servings

1 to 2 tablespoons avocado or non-GMO sunflower oil

½ dried chile pepper, seeded and minced

1 small red onion, cut into thin half-moons

Sea salt

1 cup julienned burdock

1 cup julienned carrot

1 cup finely shredded green cabbage

Organic soy sauce, to taste (approx. 1 teaspoon)

1 (1-inch) piece fresh ginger, juice extracted, pulp discarded (see Cook's Tip)

Heat the oil in a deep skillet over medium-high heat. Sauté the chile for several seconds. Add the onion and a pinch of salt. Sauté until the onion is translucent, about 2 minutes.

Add the burdock along with another pinch of salt and sauté for 2 minutes more. Add the carrot with a little more salt and sauté for 1 minute. Finally, stir in the cabbage, season lightly with soy sauce, add the ginger juice, and cook, stirring frequently, until the cabbage is limp, 3 to 5 minutes. The vegetables will be tender, with some crunch, when the dish is ready. Serve immediately.

COOK'S TIP: *To grate ginger, you will need a microplane or a ginger grater (a porcelain grater with a moat around the edges). Simply rub the ginger along the tongs to produce pulp, which will yield its juice as you grate. If you use a microplane, be sure to grate over a bowl. Once you have grated the amount you need, squeeze the pulp with your fingers to extract the juice. You may add the pulp to the dish as well, but I don't care for the texture it adds, so I always discard it. And remember, there's no need to peel ginger before use, but if you choose to, use the back of a teaspoon to pull the tissue-like skin from the pulp. A 1-inch piece of ginger will yield about 1 teaspoon of juice.*

WINTER VEGETABLE SALAD

There's nothing like roasted root veggies for strength and their incomparable sweet taste. Roasting brings the vegetables' natural sugars to the surface, resulting in sweet, succulent, satisfying flavor. But don't let their tenderness fool you—roasting also gives us incredible endurance and keeps us toasty warm. Try this twist on roasted veggies for yet another way to enjoy their brilliance.

Makes 3 to 4 servings

1 pound Brussels sprouts, left whole, stem ends trimmed
1 small daikon, cut into spears 2 inches long, ½ inch thick (about 2 cups)
2 cups whole baby carrots
3 to 4 stalks celery, cut into 2-inch spears
3 to 4 medium shallots, left whole, peeled
Organic soy sauce, to taste
2 teaspoons avocado oil
Grated zest of 1 lemon

LEMON-GINGER VINAIGRETTE

1 (1-inch) piece fresh ginger, juice extracted, pulp discarded (see Cook's Tip, page 54)
Juice of 1 lemon
¼ cup brown rice vinegar
1 tablespoon brown rice syrup
1 teaspoon umeboshi or red wine vinegar
¼ cup toasted sesame oil

Preheat the oven to 375°F.

Toss the vegetables together in a large mixing bowl. Drizzle lightly with the soy sauce and oil and stir gently to coat. Add the lemon zest and stir gently.

Spoon the vegetables into a shallow baking dish, avoiding overlap. Cover and bake for 30 minutes. Remove the cover and continue roasting until just tender—do not overcook. Aim for a slightly al dente texture that will allow the veggies to hold up in a salad.

While the vegetables are roasting, prepare the vinaigrette: In a small bowl, combine the ginger juice, lemon juice, brown rice vinegar, brown rice syrup, umeboshi (or red wine) vinegar, and sesame oil. Whisk to combine well and set aside for a few minutes to allow the flavors to develop.

When the vegetables are tender and lightly browned, gently transfer them to a mixing bowl. Drizzle lightly with the dressing and toss gently to coat. Serve warm.

NEW POTATO SALAD

There's something very "game day" about potato salad. This beauty will win you raves on your buffet table, and your friends will never guess just how healthy it really is.

Makes 4 to 6 servings

2 pounds new potatoes, unpeeled, cut into ½-inch cubes
Sea salt
1 small red onion, finely diced
3 to 4 tablespoons capers, drained (do not rinse)
12 to 16 cherry tomatoes, halved

DRESSING

⅔ cup extra-virgin olive oil
3 to 4 shallots, finely diced
¼ cup balsamic vinegar
Juice of ½ lemon
2 teaspoons brown rice syrup
3 to 4 sprigs fresh flatleaf parsley, finely minced
2 to 3 stalks fresh basil, leaves removed, finely diced

1 to 2 basil sprigs, for garnish
Sea salt

Bring a large pot of water to a boil. Add the potatoes and a pinch of salt and cook until just tender, 12 to 15 minutes. Drain and transfer to a mixing bowl. Mix in the red onion and capers, then gently fold in the tomatoes. Set aside.

To make the dressing: Place the olive oil and shallots in a small saucepan and cook over low heat for 3 to 4 minutes, until the shallots are softened. Remove from the heat and whisk in the balsamic vinegar, lemon juice, brown rice syrup, parsley, and basil. Season with salt to taste, keeping in mind the salty flavor of the capers. Allow the dressing to cool for about 3 minutes before gently tossing it with the potatoes. Serve warm, garnished with whole basil sprigs.

SWEET AND SAVORY BRUSSELS SPROUTS

This beautifully simple, light vegetable stew won't leave you feeling tired and lethargic. Made from vegetables that grow close to the ground, this dish helps you feel calm and centered, strong and sure.

Makes 3 to 4 servings

6 to 8 pearl onions or shallots, peeled and left whole

10 to 12 small Brussels sprouts, left whole, stem ends trimmed

6 to 8 unsweetened dried cherries, soaked for 15 minutes in warm water

½ cup organic corn kernels (fresh or frozen)

Organic soy sauce, to taste

1 teaspoon kuzu root or arrowroot powder, dissolved in a small amount of cold water

In a deep saucepan, layer the onions, followed by the Brussels sprouts. Drain the cherries, reserving the soaking liquid, and add them to the pot. Top with the corn kernels. Pour in enough cherry soaking water to just cover the bottom of the pot. Sprinkle with the soy sauce, then cover and bring to a gentle boil over medium-low heat.

Reduce the heat to low and simmer until the sprouts are tender, about 25 minutes. Season lightly with a little more soy sauce and simmer, covered, for 5 minutes more. Stir in the dissolved kuzu (or arrowroot) powder until a thin glaze forms over the veggies. Serve warm.

COOK'S TIP: *Use any unsweetened dried fruit in this dish if you can't get cherries.*

COOK'S TIP: *To peel pearl onions, trim the ends, blanch in boiling water for 1 minute, and cool just enough so you can handle them. Then simply pop them out of their skins. You can also buy frozen, peeled pearl onions.*

SWEET NISHIME SQUASH

Stewing vegetables creates a calm, centered energy that is without compare; stewing sweet vegetables that grow close to the ground also relaxes our stressed-out psyches. Sweet winter squash, such as butternut, acorn, hokkaido, red kuri, and kabocha, relaxes the middle of the body, satisfies the desire for a sweet taste, and warms you up on chilly days.

Makes 3 to 4 servings

1 (1-inch) piece kombu
1 dried shiitake mushroom, soaked in water until tender, stem removed
1 sweet onion, cut into thick wedges
1 small winter squash (about 1 pound), unpeeled and seeded, cut into 1-inch dice
2 tablespoons mirin
Organic soy sauce, to taste

Place the kombu and the whole shiitake mushroom in a heavy pot. Top with the onion, then layer on the squash. Add the mirin along with just enough spring or filtered water to cover the bottom of the pot. Cover and bring to a gentle boil.

Reduce the heat to low and simmer until the squash is soft, about 25 minutes. Season lightly with soy sauce and cook, uncovered, over medium heat until any remaining liquid has been absorbed and a thin, syrupy sauce has formed. Remove the kombu and shiitake and dice. Return them to the pot and stir gently to combine. Serve warm.

COOK'S TIP: *The key to this dish is to cook with as little added liquid as possible, which allows the vegetables to cook in their own juices. As you simmer, periodically check the dish to see if you need to add a bit more liquid. Don't stir; gently move a small section of the vegetables to check for liquid. Add only small amounts at a time or you will end up with soup.*

MUSTARD-PICKLED SWEET VEGETABLES

Fermented foods have finally come into their own. Their value to our wellness is without measure. They create great digestive fortitude by providing live bacteria that are essential to the health of the flora and villi that reside in our intestines. And strong intestines mean "guts"—the strength of character that we all need to face life's challenges.

Makes 1 quart

2 to 3 cucumbers, unpeeled and quartered lengthwise

⅓ head cauliflower, separated into small florets

½ small daikon, cut into ½-inch-thick, 3-inch-long spears

1 medium carrot, cut into ½-inch-thick, 3-inch-long spears

1 red onion, cut into thick half-moons

½ cup plus 1 teaspoon sea salt, divided

1 cup brown rice syrup

1 cup umeboshi or red wine vinegar

1 cup brown rice vinegar

5 to 6 tablespoons whole wheat pastry or sprouted whole wheat flour

3 tablespoons powdered mustard

Wash the vegetables very well before slicing to avoid spoilage. Mix the cut vegetables with ½ cup of the salt in a large bowl and toss to coat. Add enough spring or filtered water to cover. Stir gently to dissolve the salt. Cover and refrigerate overnight.

Drain the vegetables, rinse well, and drain again. It's important to rinse the vegetables thoroughly to remove a good amount of the salt. Set aside.

Mix the rice syrup, umeboshi (or red wine) vinegar, and brown rice vinegar in a large, heavy saucepan and cook over medium heat, stirring often, until the rice syrup is thoroughly dissolved, about 3 minutes. Set aside in the saucepan to cool.

When the vinegar mixture has cooled to room temperature, return it to the stove over medium heat and whisk in the flour, mustard, and remaining 1 teaspoon of salt. Bring the mixture to a boil over medium heat, stirring frequently to prevent lumps. Stir in the vegetables, reduce the heat to low, and simmer for 20 to 25 minutes. Transfer the entire mixture to a large bowl and cover. Refrigerate for 6 to 8 hours or overnight. To serve right away, simply drain and transfer the vegetables to a serving platter. To store, seal the vegetables and their liquid in a clean, quart-size jar and refrigerate. These pickles will keep, refrigerated, in a sealed jar, for about 2 weeks. You should eat only a small amount of pickles each day.

SPICY ASIAN COLESLAW

You're going to love this new twist on an old-fashioned favorite—coleslaw! Gone is the heavy creamy dressing. The mild character of green cabbage relaxes the middle of the body, aiding digestion and helping you manage stress. The deeply rooted energy of carrot will draw the essence of the dish deep into the body, providing strength. The cucumber cools and refreshes, and the spicy dressing moves your body's energy and gives you sparkle.

Makes 4 to 5 servings

SLAW

2 to 3 cups finely shredded
    green cabbage
1 carrot, finely julienned
12 to 15 snow peas, strings
    removed and left whole
1 small English cucumber,
    peeled, very thinly sliced
½ small head radicchio,
    finely shredded
2 to 3 fresh scallions,
    finely minced

LEMON-SPICE DRESSING

2 to 3 tablespoons
    extra-virgin olive oil
Juice of 1 lemon
1 teaspoon champagne
    vinegar
1 teaspoon powdered
    mustard
1 teaspoon powdered
    ginger
1 teaspoon brown
    rice syrup
½ to 1 teaspoon white miso

Small handful sliced
    almonds, lightly toasted,
    for serving

To make the slaw: Bring a pot of lightly salted water to a boil and cook the cabbage until crisp-tender, about 1 minute. Drain well. Blanch the carrot in the same water, keeping it still crisp, about 30 seconds. Finally, cook the snow peas until bright green, about 1 minute.

In a large mixing bowl, combine the cabbage, carrot, and snow peas with the cucumber, radicchio, and scallions.

To make the dressing: Whisk together the olive oil, lemon juice, champagne vinegar, powdered mustard, powdered ginger, brown rice syrup, and miso until well combined. Adjust the seasonings to taste, making it a little sharper, sweeter, or spicier, depending on your preference.

Mix the dressing into the vegetables and allow to stand for 10 to 15 minutes before serving to allow the flavors to develop. Just before serving, stir in the sliced, toasted almonds. Serve warm or chilled.

BRUSSELS SPROUTS WITH SHIITAKE, DAIKON, AND BABY CARROTS

In this settling dish, Brussels sprouts relax the middle organs, making you feel calm and centered. Daikon and shiitake team up to cleanse the blood and various organ systems, so they can do their jobs efficiently, which calms the body. The baby carrots provide relaxing sweetness, but their rooted nature will make you feel strong and centered. And the ginger aids circulation, promoting efficient body function and vitality.

Makes 3 to 4 servings

3 to 4 pearl onions
    or shallots, peeled
    and halved
10 to 12 baby carrots
10 to 12 Brussels sprouts,
    left whole, stem
    ends trimmed
1 cup sliced fresh daikon,
    cut into ¼-inch thick
    half-moons
4 to 5 dried shiitake
    mushrooms, soaked
    in water until tender,
    stemmed, and
    thinly sliced
Organic soy sauce, to taste
Dash mirin (optional)
1 (½-inch) piece fresh
    ginger, juice extracted,
    pulp discarded (see
    Cook's Tip, page 54)
1 teaspoon kuzu root or
    arrowroot powder,
    dissolved in a small
    amount of cold water

Layer the onions, baby carrots, sprouts, daikon, and shiitakes in a deep saucepan. Add a scant ¼ inch of spring or filtered water to the bottom of the pot. Add a splash of soy sauce and mirin (if using), cover, and bring to a gentle boil over medium heat.

Reduce the heat to low and simmer until the carrots are tender, about 25 minutes. Season lightly with a little more soy sauce and add the ginger juice. Simmer for 3 to 5 minutes more. Stir in the dissolved kuzu/arrowroot until a clear, thin glaze forms over the cooked veggies. Serve warm.

CARROTS OSSO BUCO

You may be wondering, "What is she thinking? Isn't osso buco some meat shank that's slow-roasted?" It usually is. But these slow-roasted carrots are so satisfying, you won't miss the meat.

Makes 3 to 4 servings

3 ounces dried porcini mushrooms, soaked in water until tender

2 tablespoons vegan butter substitute

6 large shallots, peeled and thinly sliced

Sea salt

6 large carrots, cut into 2-inch coins

1 cup red wine

Cracked black pepper

Preheat the oven to 350°F.

Drain the porcini mushrooms, reserving the soaking water, and coarsely chop.

Place the vegan butter in a skillet over medium heat and sauté the shallots until translucent, about 3 minutes. Add the porcini and a pinch of salt and sauté for 1 minute. Add the carrot chunks and cook, stirring occasionally, until the carrots begin to braise, about 6 minutes.

Transfer the carrot mixture to a baking dish. Add the red wine and 2 to 3 tablespoons of the porcini soaking water. Sprinkle lightly with salt and pepper and stir to combine. Cover tightly with foil and bake for 1 hour. Remove the foil and return to the oven. Continue to cook until the carrots have browned a bit and there's very little liquid left. Remove from the oven, stir gently, and serve immediately.

VEGGIE HOT POT WITH BISCUIT TOPPING

Nothing is quite as inviting as a bubbling stew topped with flaky biscuits; it can make us feel cozy and nurtured, like snuggling in a soft quilt in front of a roaring fire. This stew creates a relaxing, nourishing energy that calms and centers the mind and provides the endurance you need to get through the day with grace.

Makes 3 to 4 servings

VEGETABLE FILLING

1 to 2 tablespoons avocado or extra-virgin olive oil

3 to 4 shallots, peeled and diced

Sea salt

2 teaspoons brown rice syrup

6 to 8 Brussels sprouts, trimmed and halved

1 small rutabaga, cut into 1-inch dice

1 small (or ½ medium) butternut squash, seeded, cut into 1-inch dice

1 cup whole peeled cooked chestnuts (see Cook's Tip)

Organic soy sauce, to taste

3 to 4 tablespoons arrowroot powder

BISCUIT TOPPING

1½ cups whole wheat pastry or sprouted wheat flour

1½ teaspoons baking powder

1 teaspoon dried basil

½ teaspoon baking soda

Pinch sea salt

2 tablespoons avocado oil, plus more for brushing biscuits

¼ cup coarsely minced walnut pieces

½ cup unsweetened almond, oat, or soy milk

Preheat the oven to 375°F.

To make the vegetable filling: Heat the oil in a deep skillet over medium heat. Sauté the shallots with a pinch of salt until translucent, 2 to 3 minutes. Add the brown rice syrup and simmer over low heat, uncovered, stirring occasionally, for 2 to 3 minutes, until the shallots are caramelized.

Stir in the Brussels sprouts, rutabaga, squash, and chestnuts and cook over high heat, stirring frequently, for 2 to 3 minutes. Add enough spring or filtered water to just cover the bottom of the pan, season lightly with soy sauce, and simmer, covered, over low heat for about 10 minutes, until the vegetables are tender. Turn off the heat and gently stir in the arrowroot powder to coat. Transfer the mixture to a deep casserole dish and set aside.

To make the topping: Combine the flour, baking powder, basil, baking soda, and salt in a medium bowl. With a fork or pastry cutter, cut the oil into the flour mixture until the mixture is the texture of wet sand. Stir in the walnuts, then slowly add the milk to create a smooth dough. Cover loosely and set aside to allow the gluten to relax for 5 to 7 minutes.

Roll out the dough between two sheets of parchment (or on a floured surface) to about ½ inch thick. Cut into 2-inch rounds with a glass or biscuit cutter, taking care not to turn the cutter—just press into the dough and pull up. (Turning can take the air from the dough, making heavy biscuits.) Cover the top of the vegetable mixture with biscuits, allowing the filling to peek through. Brush the top lightly with oil and bake, covered, for 15 minutes. Uncover and bake for 15 to 20 minutes more to brown the biscuits. Serve warm.

COOK'S TIP: *To prepare the chestnuts, you have several options. Canned or frozen chestnuts are the easiest as both are fully cooked and just need to be drained or defrosted. Fresh chestnuts may be oven-baked or boiled for 25 minutes and peeled while warm. Cut a cross into the flat side of each chestnut before baking or boiling. If using dried chestnuts, soak them for 2 to 3 hours, and then pressure cook for 20 minutes—dried chestnuts will become unpleasantly grainy if boiled on the stove top, so pressure cooking is a must.*

SWEET ONION GALETTE

Sweet vegetables relax the center of the body, helping you keep your cool under fire. This richly flavored rustic tart is perfect—browned onions and delicately tart dried cherries are nestled in a flaky crust to create the perfect nourishing side dish.

Makes 4 to 6 servings

FILLING

2 to 3 tablespoons extra-virgin olive oil
6 to 8 red onions, roughly diced
Sea salt
1 cup unsweetened dried cherries, soaked in warm water for 15 minutes, drained, halved
2 tablespoons unsweetened almond, oat, or soy milk

PASTRY

1½ cups whole wheat pastry or sprouted wheat flour
1 teaspoon baking powder
¼ teaspoon sea salt
¼ cup extra-virgin olive oil
Chilled spring or filtered water

To make the filling: Heat the oil and onions in a deep skillet over medium heat. When the onions begin to sizzle, sauté with a pinch of salt until translucent, 2 to 3 minutes. Add the dried cherries and milk. Season lightly with salt and cook over medium heat, stirring occasionally, until the onions are browned and beginning to caramelize, as long as 20 minutes.

Preheat the oven to 350°F and line a baking sheet with parchment paper.

To make the pastry: Mix together the flour, baking powder, and salt in a bowl. With a fork or pastry cutter, cut in the oil until the mixture is the texture of wet sand. Slowly add up to 3 tablespoons of water to create a smooth pie dough that is not too sticky. Gather the dough into a ball, then roll it out between two sheets of parchment to create a 12-inch round.

Carefully transfer the dough to the prepared baking sheet, allowing the excess to hang over the edges. Spoon the filling onto the center of the pastry, leaving a 2-inch-wide rim of exposed dough. Fold the exposed pastry over the filling, pleating as you go, leaving the filling in the center exposed. Bake for 35 to 40 minutes, until the pastry is golden brown and firm to the touch. Remove from the oven, transfer to a serving platter, and allow to cool for 10 minutes before slicing.

COOK'S TIP: *Unsweetened dried cranberries also work well in this recipe.*

CRACKED POTATOES

If you love potatoes, this recipe is for you. The crackled skins reveal creamy, soft potato inside, making a most satisfying side dish.

Makes 4 servings

1½ **pounds red-skinned potatoes, unpeeled and rinsed well**

2 **tablespoons extra-virgin olive oil, divided**

1 **teaspoon coarse sea salt**

Generous pinch cracked black pepper

1 **tablespoon vegan butter substitute**

2 **teaspoons garlic powder**

1 **teaspoon fennel seeds, crushed**

½ **cup dry white wine**

Using the bottom of a heavy skillet, gently whack the potatoes (one at a time)—they should be flattened slightly and cracked, but still intact. Toss the potatoes with 1 tablespoon of the olive oil, sea salt, and pepper to coat.

Heat the remaining 1 tablespoon olive oil and vegan butter substitute in a 12-inch stainless steel skillet over medium-high heat until the butter is melted. Add the potatoes in a single layer. Reduce the heat to medium and cook, without moving the potatoes, until they are well browned, 6 to 8 minutes. Flip the potatoes only once, and continue cooking without stirring or moving the potatoes for another 5 minutes to ensure even browning.

Add the garlic powder and fennel seeds and cook, shaking the pan constantly, until the spices are fragrant, about 1 minute. Add the wine, cover, and reduce the heat to medium-low. Cook until the potatoes are tender and the liquid has nearly evaporated, about 8 minutes, flipping the potatoes once halfway through cooking.

Slide the potatoes onto a serving plate and scrape any remaining liquid and spices over the top.

COOK'S TIP: *Use a skillet with a tight-fitting lid so your liquid doesn't evaporate too quickly, leaving you with scorched potatoes. If you need to add a small amount of water while cooking, add it 2 tablespoons at a time.*

COOK'S TIP: *Crush fennel seeds in a mortar and pestle or by gently pressing with a chef's knife.*

STIR-FRIED CAULIFLOWER AND MUSTARD GREENS IN LEMON-SESAME SAUCE

The mild character of cauliflower is the perfect complement to the strong flavor of mustard greens. Rich in calcium and iron, mustard greens have a sharp taste that helps support the work of your liver as it metabolizes macronutrients and aids the body in ridding itself of toxins.

Makes 3 to 4 servings

STIR-FRY

1 tablespoon avocado or extra-virgin olive oil

1 small leek, split lengthwise and rinsed well, cut into 1-inch slices

2 to 3 garlic cloves, crushed and minced

Grated zest of 1 lemon

Organic soy sauce, to taste

½ head cauliflower, cut into small florets

1 bunch mustard greens, rinsed well and sliced into bite-size pieces

LEMON-SESAME SAUCE

¼ cup sesame tahini

¼ teaspoon organic soy sauce

½ teaspoon brown rice vinegar

1 teaspoon brown rice syrup

Juice of 1 lemon

Small handful black sesame seeds, lightly toasted, for garnish

To make the stir-fry: Heat the oil in a deep skillet or wok over medium-high heat. Stir-fry the leek, garlic, and lemon zest with a splash of soy sauce until the leeks are wilted, 1 to 2 minutes. Add the cauliflower and another splash of soy sauce and stir-fry for 2 to 3 minutes. Add the greens, season lightly once more with soy sauce, and stir-fry until the greens are just wilted and a rich, deep green.

To make the sauce: In a small bowl, whisk the tahini, soy sauce, brown rice vinegar, brown rice syrup, and lemon juice until smooth and creamy, adjusting the seasoning to your taste. Just before serving, stir the lemon-sesame sauce into the cooked vegetables. Garnish with the sesame seeds and serve immediately.

SPICY SAUTÉED COLLARD GREENS

Sautéing leafy green vegetables enhances their ability to make us feel vital and strong. Greens provide lots of nutrition and have been linked to helping create cardiovascular flexibility, as does cooking with extra-virgin olive oil.

Makes 3 to 4 servings

1 tablespoon extra-virgin olive oil
1 red onion, cut into thin half-moons
½ dried chile pepper, seeded, finely minced
Sea salt
1 bunch collard greens, rinsed, thinly sliced
1 lemon, quartered, for serving

Heat the oil, onion, and chile pepper in a skillet over medium heat. When the onion begins to sizzle, add a pinch of salt and sauté until translucent, 2 to 3 minutes. Add the collards, season lightly with salt, and cook, stirring constantly, until the greens are just limp and a rich, deep green, 2 to 3 minutes. Serve with lemon wedges to help your body digest the oil.

WATERCRESS, PEAR, AND PECAN SALAD WITH CANDIED CRANBERRIES

This salad is a symphony of flavors and energies. The delicate peppery taste of watercress is the perfect backdrop to the sweet pears and cranberries, nutty pecans, and sweetly spicy mustard dressing. A great starter or side course, this dish will leave your guests feeling chatty and vital, with the light freshness of the greens supporting the sweet relaxation of the pears and berries. Add the nuts and dressing and you create a social energy that will make any dinner party a hit.

Makes 4 servings

SALAD

1 to 2 bunches watercress, rinsed, left whole

2 ripe pears

3 to 4 tablespoons mirin

1 cinnamon stick

⅔ cup pecan pieces, lightly toasted

CANDIED CRANBERRIES

1 cup unsweetened dried cranberries

2 to 3 tablespoons brown rice syrup

Grated zest of 1 orange

Pinch sea salt

1 teaspoon fresh orange juice

DRESSING

¼ cup extra-virgin olive oil

3 tablespoons red wine vinegar

2 teaspoons stone-ground mustard

1 tablespoon brown rice syrup

Pinch sea salt

To make the salad: Hand-tear the watercress and arrange on 4 individual salad plates (or 1 platter).

Halve and seed the pears. Arrange the cut halves in a deep skillet with about ¼ inch of spring or filtered water. Add the mirin and cinnamon stick, cover, and bring to a gentle boil over medium heat. Reduce the heat to low and simmer until the pears are tender but not mushy, 15 to 20 minutes. Remove the pears from the liquid and set them aside to cool.

To make the cranberries: Heat the cranberries, rice syrup, orange zest, and salt in a small saucepan over medium heat. Cook until the syrup foams. Stir in the orange juice, transfer the berries to a small plate, and set aside.

To make the dressing: Warm the olive oil in a saucepan over low heat for 2 to 3 minutes, then transfer to a bowl and whisk it together with the red wine vinegar, mustard, brown rice syrup, and salt. Adjust the seasoning to your taste.

To serve the salad, take each pear half and create a fan—slice the half thinly, leaving the top ½ inch of each pear piece intact. Press gently to fan the pieces. Place on top of the watercress. Surround each pear with toasted pecan pieces and candied cranberries. Just before serving, spoon some dressing over the salad. Serve immediately.

WARM ESCAROLE AND SHIITAKE SALAD

Escarole is a delicate bitter green that aids liver function and helps sharpen your focus. Shiitake mushrooms cleanse the blood, reduce blood pressure, and lower cholesterol to keep your brain well fed by oxygen and your liver functioning optimally. Seems like a win-win to me.

Makes 3 to 4 servings

SALAD

2 teaspoons extra-virgin olive oil

1 red onion, cut into thin half-moons

½ teaspoon chili powder

Sea salt

5 to 6 dried shiitake mushrooms, soaked in water until tender, stemmed, and thinly sliced

3 to 4 tablespoons white wine

1 head escarole, rinsed well, sliced into 1-inch pieces

DRESSING

Juice of ½ lemon

2 tablespoons balsamic vinegar

2 teaspoons brown rice syrup

2 teaspoons sesame tahini

1 teaspoon red wine vinegar

½ teaspoon sea salt

To make the salad: Heat the oil and onion in a deep skillet over medium heat. When the onion begins to sizzle, add the chili powder and a pinch of salt and cook, stirring, until translucent, about 2 minutes. Add the shiitakes and another pinch of salt, followed by the white wine. Cover and cook for 3 to 4 minutes. Add the escarole, season lightly with salt, and sauté until wilted and deep green, 3 to 4 minutes.

To make the dressing: In a small bowl, whisk the lemon juice, balsamic vinegar, brown rice syrup, tahini, red wine vinegar, and sea salt until smooth and well combined. Adjust the seasonings to your taste.

Mix the dressing into the hot escarole, transfer to a serving platter, and serve immediately.

TOMATO TARTE TATIN

This impressive side dish or starter course is dramatic, absolutely beautiful, and so sweet you'll mistake it for dessert. You won't believe how easy it is to make something this pretty. Just try it! Choose a variety of colors in your cherry tomatoes for maximum visual impact.

Makes 6 to 8 servings

FILLING

2 tablespoons extra-virgin olive oil, plus more for the skillet
2 medium red onions, diced
Sea salt
1½ pounds small cherry tomatoes, left whole
2 teaspoons balsamic vinegar
Grated zest of 1 lemon
1 to 2 tablespoons arrowroot powder (optional; see Cook's Tip)

PIE CRUST

1½ cups whole wheat pastry or sprouted whole wheat flour
Pinch sea salt
2 tablespoons extra-virgin olive oil
Chilled spring or filtered water

Preheat the oven to 400°F and lightly oil a large, oven-safe skillet.

To make the filling: While the oven is warming, place the skillet over medium heat with the olive oil and onions. When the onions begin to sizzle, add a pinch of salt and cook, stirring frequently, until the onions are deeply golden and caramelized, 10 to 15 minutes. Remove from the heat.

Spread the onions evenly over the bottom of the skillet, and top them with the tomatoes, covering the onions completely. Sprinkle with sea salt, balsamic vinegar, and lemon zest.

To make the crust: Combine the flour and salt in a mixing bowl. Mix in the oil with a pastry blender or fork until the mixture is the texture of wet sand. Slowly add cold water, a tablespoon at a time, until the dough gathers into a ball. It should be not too sticky, but not too dry—the ideal dough will be moist but will not stick to your hands.

Roll the dough out between two sheets of parchment until it is 1 inch larger than the skillet, then carefully drape it over the tomato mixture. Cut off any excess crust, leaving an edge of ¼ inch. Fold this inward and crimp all the way around to form a decorative rim of crust. Cut a few decorative slits in the crust to release steam. Bake on the center rack of the oven until the crust is deeply golden and the tomatoes are bubbling, 25 to 30 minutes. Cool for about 5 minutes. Run a sharp knife around the rim of the skillet to loosen the crust. Place a plate that is slightly larger than the skillet over the tatin and carefully invert it onto the plate (replacing any tomatoes and onions that might stick on top). Serve warm, sliced into wedges. You may also serve the tatin right from the skillet, slicing it into wedges.

SESAME HIZIKI SALAD

Hiziki is so nutrient-packed, I call it rocket fuel in a cup. Loaded with calcium, vitamin C, iron, folic acid, magnesium, and other vitamins and minerals, hiziki helps create strong bones, lustrous hair, healthy blood, and smooth organ function. In this salad, hiziki's strong flavor is complemented by the rich sesame dressing.

Makes 3 to 4 servings

SALAD

1 teaspoon avocado oil
½ cup dried hiziki, rinsed
   2 to 3 times, soaked
   in water for 5 minutes,
   until tender, and drained
Organic soy sauce, to taste
Mirin, to taste
½ small leek, rinsed well
   and thinly sliced
1 carrot, julienned
1 cup julienned
   winter squash
¼ cup organic corn kernels
   (fresh or frozen)

**CREAMY SESAME
DRESSING**

¼ cup sesame tahini
Juice of 1 lemon
Juice of 1 lime
1 to 2 teaspoons brown
   rice syrup
1 teaspoon mirin
½ teaspoon soy sauce

¼ cup tan sesame seeds,
   lightly toasted,
   for garnish

To make the salad: Heat the oil in a small skillet over medium-high heat and stir in the hiziki. Season lightly with soy sauce and mirin. Spread the hiziki evenly over the skillet and add enough spring or filtered water to cover halfway. Bring to a boil, uncovered, then reduce the heat to low and simmer, covered, for 15 minutes.

Add the leek, carrot, squash, and corn. Cover and continue to simmer until the vegetables are tender, about 15 minutes more. Uncover, raise the heat to high, and cook away any remaining liquid.

To make the dressing: Whisk the tahini, lemon juice, lime juice, brown rice syrup, mirin, and soy sauce in a bowl until smooth. Add the dressing to the hiziki mixture and toss until well combined. Stir in the sesame seeds and transfer to a serving plate. Serve warm.

STEAMED GREENS MEDLEY

It doesn't get easier than this one, and the vitality this recipe provides is priceless. Leafy greens promote vascular strength, helping to create strong red blood cells; they are rich in calcium, iron, folic acid, and vitamin C. Steaming—cooking the greens in moist, hot air— maintains much of their nutritive value. Greens retain their nutrients best if cooked whole, as in this recipe, so the only time I slice them before cooking is when I'm sautéing.

Makes 3 to 4 servings

2 to 3 whole baby bok choy, rinsed well, stems trimmed

3 to 4 whole kale leaves, rinsed well

3 to 4 whole collard leaves, rinsed well

1 small bunch watercress, rinsed well

Bring about 1 inch of spring or filtered water to a boil in a deep skillet. Place a bamboo steamer over the skillet. Cook the greens separately in the order listed at left to maintain their individual characters. Cook each over high heat just until limp and richly green. Remove from the steamer and slice into bite-size pieces. Mix the greens together and serve warm, at room temperature, or lightly chilled.

COOK'S TIP: *If you don't own a bamboo steamer, use a metal steamer that sets inside a saucepan, a wire cooling rack settled over the skillet (that you cover with the skillet lid as the greens cook), or, if you have none of these tools, simply place the greens in the shallow water in the skillet, cover, and poach them until bright green.*

THE NOURISHING CYCLE

Just as life transitions smoothly through day to night, and from spring to summer to autumn to winter and back again, so does energy pass through us in an orderly, gently expanding and contracting movement, with each transformation quality nourishing the next one. This creates a smooth flow of energy through the body, resulting in efficient organ function and an overall feeling of well-being. In other words, in good health, your life force suffers no blockages; it moves freely through you, so you feel alert and vital, strong and capable.

The cycle of nourishment is simply a way to understand how one transformation of energy moves to and becomes the next. It works, again, by analogy of physical characteristics, like this: Fire burns to ash, decomposing to become (and nourish) the energy of Earth. Earth, with its gathering strength, will continue to contract until it is as hard as stone or Metal. Metal, as contracted as energy can get, has nowhere to go but to begin to expand, as all things become their opposites. Rather than explode, though, Metal energy will open up to become a gentle, floating energy, like flowing Water. Water, by its very nature, will rise as it evaporates. This ascending energy, rooted in the Earth, replicates the movement of plant growth, creating the energy known as Tree. Remember that water nourishes plants and trees naturally. Tree, in its turn, nourishes the energy transformation of Fire; you burn wood to create fire. Fire decomposes to ash, nourishing Earth, and so the cycle continues, with night turning to day and the seasons flowing from one to the next. The pulse of life continues infinitely

from one stage or transformation to the next, providing the basis of the interdependence of all living matter. If energy becomes blocked or agitated, the body will suffer an imbalance of one sort or another, with either too much or too little of any one energy. In the human body, for example, if you consume quantities of salty snacks, you overstimulate Water energy (where "salty" taste resides), resulting in overactive kidneys and bladder. However, Water energy transports life force to the liver and gallbladder, so an overstimulation of Water energy, while overworking the kidneys and bladder, will also result in the liver (Tree energy) becoming overtaxed, since Water nourishes Tree. The initial symptoms manifest as irritability and short-temperedness. If the kidneys continue to be overstimulated, they weaken, making you timid, anxious, and tired. Over time, as the liver continues to be overworked, it becomes tired, resulting in dizziness, vision disorders, muscle and tendon pain, and an overall lack of vitality with a tendency toward impatience.

Ideally though, good health is maintained when each of the Five

Transformations of Energy are evenly nourishing each other actively, assisted by our food and lifestyle choices. We must nourish each stage, but we must also be conscious of the flow of energy to maintain balance. To do so, we must be aware of the influences that each transformation has on its counterpart. We will explore these influences as we learn about The Controlling Cycle (page 130).

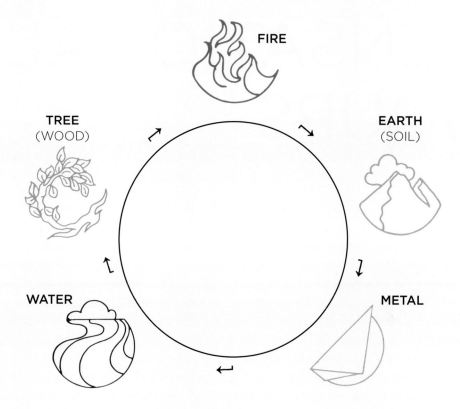

FIRE

TREE
(WOOD)

EARTH
(SOIL)

WATER

METAL

CHAPTER 4

SENSATIONAL SOUPS

I like to think of soup as bringing balance to a meal. You may also consider it the opening act. As the first course of a meal, soup introduces food to the body, setting the tone for the meal and creating the appetite for the rest of your feast. The taste, texture, flavor, fragrance, and ingredients should all complement the other dishes served. If a meal is light and simple, then a creamy, rich, hearty soup is appropriate. If the meal is rich and substantial, a lighter soup, a clear broth, or a simple vegetable soup or consommé will work toward achieving balance.

In a similar manner, ingredients, cutting techniques, and cooking styles are altered seasonally. Cool or cold weather makes hearty soups and stews, thick with grains and beans and laden with chunky root vegetables, a natural choice. Warm, humid, or hot weather calls for lighter, fresher soups when light leafy greens, shiitake mushrooms, and delicately sliced vegetables, all mildly seasoned, have the most appeal.

Soup relaxes the digestive tract so we digest our meal efficiently. Soups also help us eat less and feel satisfied longer.

In my kitchen, soup is made fresh daily, using a variety of seasonal vegetables, whole grains, and beans to ensure the best flavor and the most vitality. The quality of your soup depends on the quality of ingredients used. It's completely simple to create soups that will make you swoon, dragging your bread through the empty bowl to grab every last savory drop.

Although I use vegetable stock on occasion, I don't make it a habit. I think that simply using water makes a light, fresh soup. If you choose to make stock, however, the same rules apply: use only the freshest ingredients—no stale vegetable bits or onion skins—so your stock has great flavor.

Soup seasoning varies. Miso creates a rich, full-bodied flavor and improves digestion. Miso is a dark puree made from soybeans, barley, or rice, combined with sea salt (inhibiting the growth of undesirable bacteria), and koji, a cultured rice that stimulates fermentation. The resulting paste is aged in wooden kegs from three months to several years. A staple in Asian cuisine, miso has become increasingly familiar in Western cooking. Treasured in Asia for containing living enzymes that strengthen digestion, improve the quality of the blood, and provide a nutritious balance of complex carbohydrates, essential oils, protein, vitamins, and minerals, miso is more than just a way to flavor broth. Asian legend tells us that miso was given to humanity by the gods to ensure health and happiness. Whether this is true or not, it lends a subtle "umami" flavor to soups (and sauces and pickles). Available in a variety of flavors, miso is a bit salty and should be used lightly, usually at a ratio of 1 teaspoon per cup of liquid. Excessive miso consumption will create a counterbalancing craving for sweet tastes and liquids, so use it moderately for the best health.

Clear soups are traditionally made from a light broth made with kombu, shiitake mushrooms, or other vegetables and seasoned with soy sauce or sea salt. Mild in flavor and made with simple ingredients, like a few vegetables or cubes of tofu, clear soup is a perfect starter for a heavy meal.

Dashi, a tamari or soy sauce stock, is the basis for a full-bodied broth. Usually laced through with delicately cut vegetables, tiny cubes of tofu, and maybe some sea vegetables, this delicious type of soup is often served with cooked noodles in it.

Soup is a great way to use up leftover cooked grains or beans, or even fully cooked dishes like vegetable stews. Simply combine the ingredients with some freshly sautéed vegetables to create flavor, then season to taste with salt or miso and fresh herbs, and you'll have a richly flavored soup in no time flat. And you won't be tossing leftovers, so you'll be limiting food waste.

The varieties of soups you can make are limited only by what you can imagine. Grain soups, bean soups, vegetable soups, noodles in broth, and simple consommé broths are just the beginning. By varying the grains, beans, vegetables, cutting techniques, and cooking styles—from simmering to sautéing to pressure cooking—you can combine your choice of ingredients to create all kinds of delicious soups. Get creative, and go for it!

My soups are always simple and to the point. I start almost all of them the same way, with a mirepoix (or soffrito) of aromatic vegetables—diced onion, celery, and carrot. I may add garlic or not. I may switch it up and use leeks or shallots in place of the onion. I then add other vegetables as I like. I love a hearty soup with lots of stuff in it, so once I've made my base, I will add two or three more diced seasonal vegetables.

I may not always begin a soup with a sauté, but when I use a mirepoix as my base, I always sauté in a bit of great olive oil, taking the time to sauté each vegetable separately, not all at once. I begin with onions and a pinch of salt, cooking until they're translucent. Then I add celery and another pinch of salt. Finally, I add the carrot and a pinch of salt. This simple process is how I avoid the need for stock, by creating depth of flavor, with each vegetable holding onto its own character. Then I add the balance of my veggies, again, separately, with a pinch of salt for each, and I am in business. I add spring or filtered water, along with my grains and/or beans if I'm using them. I bring my soups to a boil loosely covered, but cook them fully covered, so I don't lose any nutrients or flavor to steam, simmering until all the ingredients are tender. Then I season to taste and simmer for a few more minutes to allow the salt to blend into the soup. Finally, I serve it garnished abundantly with fresh herbs or finely sliced leafy greens to add freshness. Every now and then, I might also add a squirt of fresh lemon juice to brighten a sweet soup, like winter squash or parsnip bisque.

Soups provide an ideal way to rebalance and strengthen the health and wellness of your kidneys, bladder, and reproductive system. Governed by the transformation of Water, this fluid energetic quality is just what the doctor ordered for your overworked and underpaid kidneys. It's why we find soup so comforting and de-stressing. Our kidneys relax and do their jobs more effectively when they're treated to a warm bowl of soup.

Read the recipes, study the techniques, master the basics, and then just do it. Make soup—or, better yet, *create* soup.

SQUASH AND SWEET CORN CHOWDER

A calming, sweetly satisfying starter course, this creamy, rich bisque is laced through with sweet corn. It's the perfect soup to transition from the intense heat of summer to the brisk, chilly days of autumn. Warming winter squash will relax your middle organs, while the sunny yellow corn keeps the memories of summer alive.

Makes 3 to 4 servings

½ small leek, rinsed well and diced
1 cup cubed, seeded butternut squash
2 cups spring or filtered water
2 cups unsweetened almond, rice, or soy milk
1 tablespoon sweet white miso
1 cup organic corn kernels (fresh or frozen)
3 to 4 sprigs fresh flatleaf parsley, coarsely chopped, for serving

Layer the leek and then the squash in a soup pot. Add the water, cover, and bring to a boil over medium heat. Add the milk, cover, and reduce the heat to low. Simmer until the squash is quite soft, about 35 minutes.

Puree the soup in batches using a food mill or in a food processor. Return the soup to the pot over low heat and bring it back to a simmer. Remove a small amount of liquid and use it to dissolve the miso. Stir the miso mixture and corn gently into the pot and simmer for 3 to 4 minutes to activate the enzymes in the miso. Serve hot, garnished with parsley.

SWEET WINTER SQUASH BISQUE

There is nothing quite like winter squash for delicate sweetness. Growing close to the ground, winter squash stabilizes blood sugar and relaxes the body's middle organs—the spleen, pancreas, and stomach—which can improve digestion and create a calm, centered feeling within.

Makes 3 to 4 servings

3 cups plus 3 tablespoons spring or filtered water, divided

1 small onion, finely diced

Sea salt

5 cups small cubed winter squash

1 to 2 parsnips, small roll cut

1 to 2 cups unsweetened almond, rice, or soy milk

2 to 3 tablespoons mirin or white wine

1 to 2 scallions, thinly sliced on the diagonal, for serving

Heat 3 tablespoons of the water in a soup pot over medium heat. Add the onion and a pinch of salt and sauté for 2 minutes. Add the squash, parsnips, remaining 3 cups water, milk, mirin (or white wine), and a light sprinkling of salt. Bring to a boil over medium heat, covered. Reduce the heat to low and simmer for 20 minutes. Season lightly with salt to taste so that the soup tastes sweet, then continue to simmer, covered, until the squash is quite soft, about 15 minutes.

Puree the soup in batches in a food mill or a food processor fitted with the metal blade. Return the soup to the pot and warm over low heat for 2 to 3 minutes to allow the flavors to develop. Serve hot, garnished with scallions.

HEARTY LENTIL SOUP WITH FRESH HERBS

Bean soups are brilliant. They are a great source of protein, and they provide us with tremendous endurance and stamina. Put that together with the relaxing energy of soup, and you have the winning combination of a clear head and incredible staying power.

Makes 3 to 4 servings

1 tablespoon extra-virgin olive oil
1 small red onion, finely diced
Sea salt
2 garlic cloves, crushed and minced
1 to 2 stalks celery, finely diced
1 carrot, finely diced
1 cup dried green or brown lentils, sorted and rinsed
1 (1-inch) piece kombu or 1 bay leaf
4 to 5 cups spring or filtered water
½ cup organic corn kernels (fresh or frozen)
1 tablespoon barley miso
3 to 4 stems flatleaf parsley, minced
2 to 3 stems fresh basil, leaves removed, shredded
1 to 2 stalks fresh rosemary, leaves removed, minced

In a soup pot, combine the olive oil, onion, and garlic over medium heat. When the onion begins to sizzle, add a pinch of salt and sauté until they are translucent, about 3 minutes. Add the celery and a pinch of salt; sauté for 1 minute. Add the carrot and a pinch of salt, and sauté for 1 minute more.

Add the lentils, kombu (or bay leaf), and water. Bring to a boil, uncovered, over medium heat. Boil for 2 to 3 minutes. Add the corn to the soup. Cover; reduce the heat to low, and simmer until the vegetables are soft, about 40 minutes. Remove a small amount of liquid and stir it together with the miso until it is dissolved. Stir the miso mixture gently into the pot and simmer gently, uncovered, for 3 to 4 minutes to activate the enzymes in the miso. Stir in the parsley, basil, and rosemary; remove the kombu (or bay leaf) and serve hot.

COOK'S TIP: *I like to make this soup in big batches because it freezes so well. I also love to make it spicy on occasion by adding crushed red pepper flakes. Err to just a pinch if you're not into spicy flavor, but if you like it, go ahead and season to taste.*

CREAMY WHITE BEAN SOUP WITH ESCAROLE

White beans have a cooling energy in the body and have been clinically proven to help reduce cholesterol and blood pressure, making them a heart-healthy powerhouse. Swirling the soup through with hearty, leafy greens prevents the soup from being too heavy; they add a light, fresh vitality, plus lots of calcium and iron.

Makes 3 to 4 servings

1 bay leaf
½ cup dried cannellini beans, sorted and rinsed
3 to 4 cups spring or filtered water
1 teaspoon extra-virgin olive oil
1 small yellow onion, finely diced
Sea salt
1 to 2 stalks celery, finely diced
2 parsnips, finely diced
1 tablespoon sweet white miso
1 cup finely diced escarole

Place the bay leaf in a soup pot. Add the beans, followed by the water, and bring to a boil, uncovered, over high heat. Boil for 5 minutes. Cover; reduce the heat to low, and simmer until soft, about 1 hour. Remove and discard the bay leaf.

Meanwhile, heat the oil and onion in a skillet over medium heat. When the onion begins to sizzle, add a pinch of salt and sauté until translucent, about 2 minutes. Add the celery and another pinch of salt; sauté for 1 to 2 minutes. Add the parsnips and another pinch of salt; sauté, stirring occasionally, until shiny with oil.

Transfer the beans and cooking liquid to a food processor fitted with the metal blade and puree until smooth. (A food mill doesn't work well here for creaminess.) Return the beans to the pot over low heat, and add a small amount of water if the bean mixture is too thick or you prefer a lighter soup. In a small bowl, dissolve the miso in a small amount of the hot bean liquid. Stir the miso mixture, sautéed vegetables, and escarole into the pot. Simmer for 3 to 4 minutes to activate the enzymes in the miso. Serve hot.

VEGETABLE SOUP WITH PESTO

I'll admit, I could eat basil pesto on just about anything, but a dollop on fresh veggie soup is just heaven to me. The light, fresh energy of the herb is a perfect complement to any hearty bean and veggie soup, preventing it from becoming heavy, sinking in the body.

Makes 3 to 4 servings

PESTO

1 cup packed fresh basil leaves
¼ cup extra-virgin olive oil
4 to 5 tablespoons lightly toasted pine nuts
1 to 2 teaspoons white miso
1 teaspoon red wine vinegar
1 teaspoon brown rice syrup

SOUP

1 small red onion, diced
½ small leek, split lengthwise, rinsed well, and diced
3 to 4 fingerling potatoes, diced
2 small carrots, diced
1 yellow summer squash, diced
1 cup cooked cannellini beans (or other white beans)
5 cups spring or filtered water
1 bay leaf
2½ teaspoons white miso
1 cup fresh green beans, trimmed and sliced on the diagonal into ½-inch pieces

To make the pesto: Blanch the basil in boiling water for 30 seconds, then drain and dry by wrapping it in a kitchen towel. This will help the pesto hold its green color. Combine the blanched basil, olive oil, pine nuts, miso, red wine vinegar, and brown rice syrup in a food processor fitted with the metal blade. Pulse to create a coarse paste. Set aside.

To make the soup: Layer the onion, leek, potatoes, carrots, and summer squash in a soup pot in the order listed. Top with the beans; add the water and bay leaf. Cover and bring to a boil over medium heat. Reduce the heat to low and simmer until the vegetables are quite soft, 20 to 25 minutes. Remove and discard the bay leaf.

Working in batches, put the soup through a food mill or puree it in a food processor to create a smooth texture. Return the soup to the pot over medium heat. Remove a small amount of liquid and stir in the miso to dissolve it. Stir the miso mixture and green beans into the soup and simmer for 3 to 4 minutes, taking care not to boil, as it will destroy the enzymes in miso that aid digestion. Serve hot, with a dollop of pesto in each bowl.

TUSCAN BREAD SOUP

This splendid soup is practically a meal in itself. It's a thick, rich stew laden with vegetables and beans, delicately seasoned . . . and there's bread "melted" into it. Is there anything more delicious?

Makes 3 to 4 servings

1 bay leaf
½ cup dried white navy beans, sorted and rinsed
4 to 5 cups spring or filtered water, divided
1 tablespoon extra-virgin olive oil
½ red onion, diced
½ small leek, split lengthwise, rinsed well, and diced
Sea salt
1 to 2 carrots, diced
1 cup diced winter squash
3 to 4 fingerling potatoes, diced
1 to 2 stalks celery, diced
1 cup diced green cabbage
1 tablespoon white miso
1 yellow summer squash, diced
1 bunch dark leafy greens, such as kale or broccoli rabe, thinly sliced
4 to 5 slices stale whole-grain sourdough bread
3 to 4 sprigs basil, leaves removed, minced, for garnish

Place the bay leaf in a heavy pot. Top with the beans and 3 cups of the water. Bring to a boil, uncovered, over high heat. Continue to boil for 5 minutes, then cover and reduce the heat to low. Simmer until the beans are just tender, about 45 minutes. Transfer the beans and any remaining cooking liquid to a bowl and mash until about half-broken. Discard the bay leaf. Set aside.

Set a soup pot over medium heat and add the olive oil, onion, and leek. When the onion begins to sizzle, add a pinch of salt and sauté until the onion is translucent, about 2 minutes. Add the carrots, winter squash, potatoes, and a pinch of salt; sauté for 1 minute. Add the celery, cabbage, and a pinch of salt, and continue to sauté until the cabbage is limp. Add the remaining 1 to 2 cups water along with the mashed beans and their liquid. Cover the pot and bring to a boil. Reduce the heat to low and simmer until the vegetables are tender and the beans are quite soft, about 30 minutes.

Remove a small amount of liquid and stir it together with the miso to dissolve. Stir the miso mixture, summer squash, and greens into the pot. Simmer, uncovered, for 3 to 4 minutes to activate the enzymes in the miso.

To assemble the soup, place a layer of bread slices on the bottom of a small soup tureen or heat-resistant casserole dish. Ladle a generous amount of soup over the bread. Repeat with another layer of bread and then soup.

Continue layering until the tureen is full, finishing with a top layer of bread. Cover the tureen and allow the soup to stand for 5 to 7 minutes before serving. Ladle soup and bread into individual serving bowls. Garnish with basil and serve hot.

COOK'S TIP: *You can layer the soup and keep it in a warm oven before serving for as long as 1 hour to "melt" the bread more.*

DAIKON-SHIITAKE CONSOMMÉ

The combination of shiitake and daikon can be instrumental in helping your body break down excess protein and fat that may have accumulated in and around various organs and systems. A consommé like this is also the perfect starter to a hearty meal. Light and fresh, this thin soup relaxes the body and aids in the digestion of rich feasts.

Makes 3 to 4 servings

4 cups spring or
    filtered water
1 (2-inch) piece kombu,
    soaked in water for 2 to
    3 minutes, until tender
3 to 4 dried shiitake
    mushrooms, soaked
    in water for 10 to 15
    minutes, until tender,
    left whole, stemmed
6 to 8 round slices fresh
    daikon, ¼ inch thick
Organic soy sauce, to taste
1 to 2 scallions, thinly
    sliced on the diagonal,
    for garnish

Place the water, kombu, and whole shiitakes in a saucepan over medium heat. Cover and bring to a boil. With the tip of a sharp knife, score each daikon round and add them to the soup. Cover, reduce the heat to low, and simmer until the mushrooms and daikon are tender, about 10 minutes. Lightly season with soy sauce; simmer for 5 minutes more. Remove the kombu and discard. Serve hot, 2 daikon and 1 shiitake per bowl, garnished with scallions.

COOK'S TIP: *When soaking kombu, allow it to stand in water just until tender. If you soak it too long, the minerals will leach into the water and the kombu will develop a slickness that will make it difficult to work with and unappealing to eat.*

PASTA E FAGIOLI

There's nothing like Italian bean soup . . . or Italian anything, in my view. This one was a religious experience in my house. My mother made it for my father every Friday. I can still see him sitting at the head of the table, with a heel of Italian bread and his big bowl of soup. The combination of beans and sautéed vegetables created the perfect balance of energy and endurance, which he sorely needed with us kids around!

Makes 3 to 4
servings

2 to 3 teaspoons extra-virgin olive oil
2 garlic cloves, smashed and minced
½ red onion, diced
Sea salt
1 stalk celery, diced
1 carrot, diced
Generous pinch dried oregano
Generous pinch rosemary
½ cup dried cannellini beans, sorted
4 cups spring or filtered water
1 bay leaf
1 cup diced tomatoes
2 small zucchini, diced
1½ cups cooked pasta, such as small shells, orzo, acini, or elbows
1 cup diced dark leafy greens, such as kale, collards, or broccoli rabe
3 to 4 sprigs fresh basil, leaves separated and minced, for serving

Heat the olive oil, garlic, and onion in a soup pot over medium heat. When the onion begins to sizzle, add a pinch of salt and sauté until translucent, about 2 minutes. Add the celery and a pinch of salt and sauté until shiny with oil. Add the carrot and another pinch of salt and sauté until shiny with oil. Add the dried herbs and beans, followed by the water, bay leaf, tomatoes, and zucchini. Cover and bring to a boil. Reduce the heat to low and cook until the beans are tender, 45 minutes to 1 hour.

When the beans are tender, season to taste with salt, and stir in the pasta and greens. Continue to simmer until the greens wilt, 2 to 3 minutes. Serve hot, garnished with basil.

COOK'S TIP: *To ensure the pasta is not mushy, cook it to 90 percent done and then stir it into the soup. In those last minutes of cooking, the pasta will be perfectly al dente.*

SUMMER VEGETABLE SOUP WITH QUINOA SALAD

This is a great summer dish—a light soup and grain meal all in one bowl. Summer vegetables have lots of moisture and keep us cool, especially when served as soup. A scoop of quinoa salad makes this the perfect summer soup, because quinoa is a whole grain that grows in a hot climate, so it cools us down. Plus it cooks quickly, so you won't create lots of heat in your kitchen. The best part is that this soup is splendidly pretty on a summer table.

Makes 3 to 4 servings

SOUP

2 teaspoons avocado or extra-virgin olive oil
½ small leek, split lengthwise, rinsed well, and thinly sliced
Sea salt
1 stalk celery, diced
1 to 2 small carrots, diced
1 small yellow summer squash, diced
4 to 5 cups spring or filtered water
2½ teaspoons white miso
1 to 2 scallions, thinly sliced on the diagonal, for serving
Fruity olive oil, for serving

QUINOA SALAD

½ cup quinoa, rinsed well
1 cup spring or filtered water
Pinch sea salt
2 scallions, diced
¼ cup organic corn kernels (fresh or frozen)
½ roasted red bell pepper, diced (see Cook's Tip, page 113)
½ teaspoon red wine vinegar
½ teaspoon balsamic vinegar

To make the soup: Heat the oil in a soup pot over medium heat. Add the leek with a pinch of salt and sauté until limp, about 1 minute. Add the celery and another a pinch of salt, and sauté until shiny with oil. Add the carrots and a pinch of salt, and sauté for 1 minute. Add the summer squash and stir until combined. Add the water, cover, and bring to a boil. Reduce the heat to low and simmer, covered, until the vegetables are quite soft, 15 to 20 minutes.

Working in batches, put the soup through a food mill to create a smooth, silky texture. Return the soup to the pot and bring it back to a simmer over low heat. Remove a small amount of liquid and use it to dissolve the miso. Stir the miso mixture into the soup; simmer for 3 to 4 minutes to activate the enzymes in the miso.

While the soup cooks, make the salad: Add the quinoa and water to a saucepan and cover loosely. Bring to a boil over medium heat. Add the salt; cover and simmer until all the liquid has been absorbed, about 17 minutes. Stir in the scallions, corn, bell pepper, red wine vinegar, and balsamic vinegar.

To serve, place a scoop of quinoa salad in the center of individual soup bowls. Ladle the soup around the salad, garnish with the scallions, and serve hot with a drizzle of a fruity olive oil.

COOK'S TIP: *To roast a bell pepper, place it directly on a high flame, turning carefully with tongs as each part of the pepper chars. When fully charred, transfer the pepper to a paper sack. Seal and allow to steam for 5 to 7 minutes. Peel away the charred skin, removing as much of the char as possible without rinsing the pepper (you will lose flavor if you rinse).*

If you have an electric stove, simply cut the pepper in half and leave the seed bed inside. Lay the pepper, cut side down, on a baking sheet and place under a broiler on high heat and char completely before placing in a paper sack.

WINTER VEGETABLE SOUP WITH MOCHI CROUTONS

When the cold winds of winter seem to blow right through you, there is nothing quite like a hearty bowl of soup to warm your shivering bones. Winter vegetables and grains come together in this hearty soup to create warmth in the middle organs of the body, giving you strength, stamina, a calm mind, and a warm body.

Makes 3 to 4 servings

SOUP

1 (½-inch) piece kombu, soaked in water until tender and diced
½ red onion, cut into large dice
1 cup diced green cabbage
1 cup cubed winter squash
⅓ cup rolled oats
4 to 5 cups spring or filtered water
2 to 3 teaspoons barley miso
2 to 3 scallions, thinly sliced on the diagonal, for serving

MOCHI CROUTONS

Avocado oil, as needed for frying
12 (½-inch) mochi cubes

To make the soup: Layer the kombu, red onion, cabbage, and winter squash in a soup pot in the order listed. Top with the oats, then add the water. Cover and bring to a boil over medium heat. Reduce the heat to low and simmer, covered, until the vegetables are soft and the oats are very creamy, 35 to 40 minutes. Remove a small amount of liquid and use it to dissolve the miso. Stir the miso mixture gently into the soup and simmer, uncovered, for 3 to 4 minutes to activate the enzymes in the miso.

To make the croutons: Just before serving, heat enough oil to generously cover the bottom of a heavy skillet over medium heat. Add the mochi and fry until golden brown on all sides, turning as they brown. Drain well on paper towels.

Serve hot, garnished with scallions and 3 to 4 mochi croutons per bowl.

COOK'S TIP: *Don't make the croutons too far in advance of serving time, or they will get oily and mushy. You want them crispy and fresh.*

COOK'S TIP: *Mochi is made from sweet brown rice and can be found in most natural foods stores, but you can also make bread croutons, using the same process above, if you don't have or can't get mochi.*

CREAMY MUSHROOM SOUP

Creamy soups are like comfort in a bowl. Laden with relaxing mushrooms, this soup helps you manage the little stresses of daily life that can sometimes be overwhelming.

Makes 3 to 4 servings

1 teaspoon extra-virgin olive oil
1 small yellow onion, diced
Sea salt
5 to 6 fresh shiitake mushrooms, stemmed and thinly sliced
1 cup thinly sliced cremini mushrooms
½ cup (1 ounce) dried maitake blooms (see Cook's Tip)
4 cups unsweetened almond, rice, or soy milk
2 teaspoons white miso
1 to 2 scallions, thinly sliced on the diagonal, for serving

Set a soup pot over medium heat and add the olive oil and onion. When the onion begins to sizzle, add a pinch of salt and sauté until translucent, 2 to 3 minutes. Add the shiitakes with a pinch of salt and sauté for 1 minute. Add the cremini and maitake mushrooms with another pinch of salt and sauté until they begin to release their juices. Add the milk, cover, and bring to a boil over medium heat. Reduce the heat to low and simmer for 30 minutes to develop the flavors.

Remove a small amount of liquid from the pot and stir it together with the miso until dissolved. Stir the miso mixture gently into the soup and simmer, uncovered, for 3 to 4 minutes to activate the enzymes in the miso. Serve hot, garnished with scallions.

COOK'S TIP: *Dried maitake mushrooms are unlike other dried mushrooms in that you do not need to reconstitute them. They cook quickly. They resemble dried flowers, so you simply break off "leaves" or "blooms" for the quantity desired. If you prefer to use fresh maitake, simply pull off the "blooms" or slice the piece of the mushroom you're using crosswise and then dice it. There is no stem to discard, so use the whole mushroom.*

CREAMY MILLET CHOWDER

I love millet—from its sunny yellow color to its creamy, comforting texture to the fact that it aids in digestion. This millet soup is more than just delicious. Its warming character and sweet vegetables relax the body and keep us warm in cool weather. This soup will enable you to face life with a calm, centered attitude.

Makes 3 to 4 servings

½ **sweet yellow onion, diced**

¼ **head green cabbage, diced**

1 **(1-inch) piece wakame, soaked in water for 2 to 3 minutes, until tender, diced**

½ **cup yellow millet, rinsed well**

4 to 5 **cups spring or filtered water**

2 **teaspoons barley miso**

½ **cup organic corn kernels (fresh or frozen)**

1 **cup diced dark leafy greens, such as kale or collards**

1 to 2 **scallions, thinly sliced on the diagonal, for serving**

Layer the onion, cabbage, wakame, and millet in a soup pot. Add the water, cover, and bring to a boil over medium-high heat. Reduce the heat to low and simmer until the vegetables are soft and the millet is creamy, about 25 minutes.

Remove a small amount of liquid from the pot and use it to dissolve the miso. Stir the miso mixture, corn, and greens into the pot and simmer for 3 to 4 minutes, uncovered, to activate the enzymes in the miso. Garnish with scallions and serve hot.

SPLIT PEA–CAULIFLOWER BISQUE

This simple, elegant soup is so richly flavored, you'll want it to be the first, main, and last course of the meal. Protein-packed, with a wee bit of curry for spice, this soup is the perfect dish for creating strong digestion.

Makes 3 to 4 servings

1 to 2 tablespoons
   avocado oil
½ yellow onion, diced
2 garlic cloves, crushed
   and minced
Sea salt
1 teaspoon curry powder
2 cups cauliflower florets
1 cup yellow or green split
   peas, rinsed well
4 cups spring or
   filtered water
2 teaspoons white miso
2 to 3 sprigs fresh flatleaf
   parsley, minced,
   for serving

Stir together the olive oil, onion, and garlic in a soup pot over medium heat. When the onion begins to sizzle, add a small pinch of salt and the curry powder and sauté until the onion is translucent, about 2 minutes. Add the cauliflower and sauté until shiny with oil. Add the split peas and water and bring to a boil. Reduce the heat to low, cover, and cook until the peas are quite soft, 45 minutes to 1 hour.

Remove a small amount of broth from the pot and use it to dissolve the miso. Return the miso mixture to the pot; using a handheld blender or food processor, puree the soup until smooth. Return to the stove to warm through and serve garnished with fresh parsley.

COOK'S TIP: *You may use either green or yellow split peas to create two different and beautiful soups.*

WINTER SQUASH, APPLE, AND FENNEL BISQUE

This soup is the epitome of autumn yumminess. With a bit of sweetness tempered by the crisp flavor of fennel, it's the perfect starter to any cool-weather feast.

Makes 3 to 4 servings

1 small winter squash (preferably butternut or red kuri), enough to yield 2 to 3 cups cubed

Extra-virgin olive oil, as needed for roasting vegetables, plus more for serving

1 fennel bulb, trimmed, diced, leafy fronds reserved for serving

2 garlic cloves, smashed and minced

Sea salt

2 Gala or Fuji apples, unpeeled, cored, and diced

3 to 4 cups spring or filtered water

2 tablespoons white miso

Preheat the oven to 400°F.

Halve the winter squash and remove the seeds. Lightly oil your hands and rub the squash halves with oil. Sprinkle the cut sides lightly with salt. Place the squash, cut side down, on a baking sheet and bake, uncovered, until fork-tender, about 40 minutes.

Combine the diced fennel and garlic with a light drizzle of olive oil and a sprinkle of salt and toss to coat. Arrange on another baking sheet and bake, uncovered (at the same time as the squash), for 30 minutes.

When the squash, fennel, and garlic are tender, transfer to a food processor or blender and puree until smooth. Add the apple and water and puree again until smooth. Add water as needed to create a thinner soup as you desire.

Transfer the soup to a saucepan and warm over low heat for 15 minutes. Remove a small amount of broth from the pot and stir it together with the miso until dissolved. Stir the miso back into the soup and simmer, taking care not to boil, for 1 to 2 minutes.

Serve garnished with fresh fennel fronds and, if desired, a light drizzle of fruity olive oil.

PAPPA AL POMODORO

Visions of a Tuscan summer come with each spoonful of this simple, richly flavored Italian tradition. Using only the freshest tomatoes at the peak of their flavor, this simple soup is summer at its best.

Makes 3 to 4 servings

1 tablespoon extra-virgin olive oil, plus more for serving

2 to 3 garlic cloves, crushed and finely minced

2 pounds vine-ripened tomatoes, diced (do not peel or seed)

3 to 4 cups spring or filtered water

1 carrot, unpeeled

Sea salt

1 small loaf whole-grain sourdough bread, coarsely crumbled

2 teaspoons sweet white miso

1 small bunch fresh basil, finely minced, for serving

Heat the olive oil and the garlic in a soup pot over medium heat. As soon as the garlic begins to sizzle (do not let it burn), add the tomatoes and water. Bring to a boil and add the whole carrot, several pinches of salt, and the bread. Stir well, cover, and return to a boil. Reduce the heat to low and simmer until the bread is quite soft, 35 to 40 minutes.

Remove the carrot from the pot and discard. Remove a small amount of broth from the pot and use it to dissolve the miso. Stir the miso mixture into the soup and simmer, uncovered, for 3 to 4 minutes to activate the enzymes in the miso. Stir in the basil and serve right away with a drizzle of fruity olive oil.

THE CONTROLLING CYCLE

Nature loves balance and so, within the Five Transformations of Energy, there is a natural controlling or limiting cycle—a system of checks and balances, if you will. In this cycle of energy movement, each stage serves to regulate and control its counterpart from becoming excessive or stagnant, holding too much energy, or depleting itself, creating deficiencies and excesses in various organ systems. This controlling aspect of the Five Transformations regulates smooth organ function, maintaining order within the grand scheme of things. Each transformation of energy has its opposing or complementary energy working to maintain balance and stability of the energy flow through the body.

It goes like this: Fire (heart and small intestine) controls Metal (lungs and large intestine) energy; remember, fire melts metal. Metal (lungs and large intestine) controls Tree (liver, gallbladder, nervous system) energy; think of an ax chopping wood. Tree (liver, gallbladder, nervous system) controls Earth (spleen, pancreas, stomach) energy; think of how plants draw nutrients from the earth. Earth (spleen, stomach, pancreas) controls Water (kidneys, bladder, reproductive system) energy; earth absorbs water, creating mud. Water (kidneys, bladder, reproductive system) controls Fire (heart, small intestine) energy; water can extinguish any flame.

Within this system of checks and balances, excessive energy can be subdued and deficient energy can be bolstered to create balance. Using both nourishing and controlling energies, you work to maintain smooth transformation of energy through your body. For example, if kidney (Water) energy is weak or depleted, you would be feeling tired and timid, with a washed-out look to your skin. To counter this, you would nourish that energy by choosing foods from the Metal character, since Metal is the supporting energy to Water. If,

however, the kidneys are overstimulated, containing an excessive amount of stimulation, you would be feeling jittery, inflexible, anxious, and unable to sleep. To settle things down, you would look to Water's complementary energy, Earth, since it has energy that can override excessive Water energy—turning water to mud, metaphorically speaking.

When applied to our bodies in daily life, the Five Transformations of Energy illuminate the way energy moves through us and how it affects each of our organs and their functions. With centuries of use, practitioners of Chinese medicine have developed an understanding of the use of food, exercise, herbs, and other specifics to maintain our health and to change and heal various conditions, restoring our vitality.

Yin and Yang . . . Five Transformations of Energy . . . Nourishing and Controlling Cycles . . . yikes! You're probably wondering what all this has to do with the quality of your daily life—and more than that, your food. Life has many ups and downs; each little adventure keeps us on our toes. If you are living in a more balanced state, these challenges are easier to handle. The way we live in the modern world violates nature at every turn. We live flat-out, all or nothing, work hard, party hard, creating chaos in the process. When we live at a crazy pace, we create erratic energy. We are constantly overscheduled and connected to devices, making balance harder to achieve.

Think of it like this: Picture yourself standing on a seesaw. Which is easier—trying to balance with your feet perched at the outer ends of the planks, or standing with your feet planted securely on either side of the center point? While there is no such thing as perfect balance (or perfect health, for that matter), you can hover closer to the center, maintaining a delicate fluctuation of movement, as you allow the world to gently expand and contract around you, with you as an integral part of it all.

You can apply this thinking to everything in your life. If you live in extremes, the body becomes exhausted. You can choose to thrash wildly between these extreme points, or you can gently rock back and forth, staying vital, and feeling alert yet calm. You can't completely avoid extremes in life. There will always be challenges like job stress, family issues, or the state of the world. Extreme living exacts a high toll, but if you live your life in a generally centered manner, taking responsibility for what you can control, you will be prepared for the roadblocks that life throws in your path.

You can't control a lot of what happens in your daily life—not the weather, or traffic, or politics, or the behavior of those around you. The one aspect of your life over which you do maintain complete and total control is your food choices. Only you decide what

to put in your mouth from moment to moment. Oh sure, you may be influenced by lots of things, including ancestry, habit, marketing and other cultural images, or convenience, but ultimately, you make conscious (or unconscious) choices regarding what you eat. And those foods you choose determine who you are, how you feel, and the health of your body.

Now before you freak out and wonder how you will ever possibly manage to consider all of this as you cook, especially if cooking is new to you, relax, baby. I've got you. In each recipe, I've worked to balance the foods, cooking styles, and seasonality to help you understand and create balance. Sure, you might have to refer to these little charts and descriptions as you familiarize yourself with this new way of looking at what you eat, but that's it. Just cook, eat, and enjoy the resulting balance in your life, and as your intuition kicks into very high gear, you'll be using these simple recipes as your jumping-off place to create your own personal masterpieces of balance.

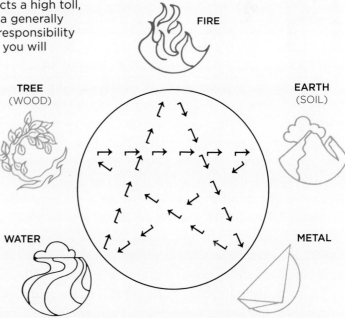

FIRE

TREE (WOOD)

EARTH (SOIL)

WATER

METAL

CHAPTER 5

WHOLE GRAINS: THE STAFF OF LIFE

Here's what you need to know about grains and their importance to our wellness: from Ceres, the Roman goddess of agriculture, sprouted the word "cereal," representing the family of grasses known to us as cereal grains, the most important food to humankind. You heard me right, *the most important food to humankind . . .* whole cereal grains.

Most grasses are perennial plants, with flowers that have no petals. Grains are the fruit as well as the seed of the plant, which means that they have within them the ability to rebuild themselves using the materials of their own construction. Wait, *what?* Cereal grains contain the most highly evolved seed of any food plant; their embryological roots, stems, and leaves have the same patterns as those of mature, fully developed plants. This developmental process mimics that of humanity: our embryo stage contains all the patterns needed for full maturity. Are you seeing the connection here?

The edible portion of grains is the kernel; it is, in reality, a complete fruit with a protective husk over it. In some grains, like rice, millet, oats, and barley, this outer shell is tough and must be removed in order to eat the seed. In the case of grains like corn and wheat, the hulls are tender and are eaten along with the fruit inside.

Grains contain the ability to reproduce in great abundance from a single seed, making them highly productive plants. Each whole cereal grain represents both the beginning and the end of the plant's life, containing within it all the potential and energy of the entire plant.

And the point, you may be wondering, that I am trying to tell you here?

Because of this unique character, grains, more than any other food, have the greatest capacity for increasing human potential on all levels of our existence. Their ability to reproduce in great quantity, with very little help or interference from us, as well as their adaptability and versatility, make grains our most valuable nourishment in my view.

I know there's debate about the value of grains, as carbohydrates have become demonized in the face of our growing obesity and diabetes epidemics and the popularity of high-protein diets, which promise slender bodies if we only eschew grains. But I think it's a critical error to turn away from the food of humanity . . . cereals.

Within the human species lie the seeds of generations to come that will shape the planet's future. Grains hold in them the evolution of past, present, and future blood quality that will determine the health of humanity. Whole grains have the ability to fine-tune the human nervous system, unifying all organ function into one smoothly operating organism.

As a result, whole grains have constituted the principal food of humanity for tens of thousands of years. Every civilization prior to ours viewed cereals as the foundation of life, developing different types of grain cultivation, farming, harvesting, and preparation, giving rise to the great diversity and rich, ethnic differences of our various cultures and cuisines. Until modern times, cooked whole grains were eaten as a primary staple food throughout the world.

Whole cereal grains provide us with a balanced, peaceful energy and lots of staying power. In their whole form, with germ, bran, and endosperm intact, whole grains are long-chain carbohydrates, which break down slowly in our bloodstream, providing long-term stamina and endurance unparalleled in other foods. This is pure energy here, but not the scrape-you-off-the-ceiling-because-you're-wound-so-tight kind of energy that simple carbohydrates and sugar provide. This is the calm, determined energy of staying power and clear-minded thinking.

In plant-passionate cooking, whole cereal grains are viewed as the cornerstone of a healthy diet. They are an essential part of our daily food and it is important, as in all aspects of cooking and nutrition, to consume a variety of grains. Don't condemn yourself to a grim existence of only short-grain brown rice, as wonderful as it is. Try lots of grains, such as millet, barley, quinoa, amaranth, teff, Job's tears, buckwheat, oats, wheat, rye, corn, farro, and wild rice. There are also polished grains, designed to lighten things up a bit, like white rice, couscous, Arborio rice, cracked wheat, rolled oats, cornmeal, corn grits, noodles, bread, and seitan, a delicious and incredibly satisfying meat alternative made from simmered wheat gluten. Are you seeing the possibilities here? You can try a new grain every day for a month and not repeat yourself! What a great adventure!

Cooking grain is as simple as the grain itself. There are a variety of methods used to prepare delicious grain dishes, but I always see the most delicious results when I cook grains in a heavy pot. You can create variety with different cooking techniques—from pressure cooking to dry roasting to boiling. You can soak grains, pan toast them before cooking, or sprout them for ease of digestion.

There's a formula for cooking most whole grains, and it's so easy, it's silly. Nearly all whole grains, with one exception, cook perfectly with two parts water to one part grain. The grains come out moist but light, not sticky or hard. Perfect. The exception is millet, which requires four to five parts water to one part grain in order to achieve its characteristic creamy consistency. Cracked grains like polenta and bulgur are different matters, with polenta requiring five parts water and grains like bulgur and couscous cooking to their best textures at a ratio of one to one.

I love to cook whole grains as morning porridge. Cooked soft, whole grains make for a soothing, comforting, stick-to-your-ribs breakfast. I add diced vegetables, organic corn, and small cubes of tofu to create variety, texture, and incredible nutrition. Cooked at a ratio of five to one, all whole grains will take on a creamy texture. Vary the veggies, vary the grains, and mix and match to create an endless array of morning feasts. Served with lightly boiled or stewed vegetables, it's a real breakfast of champions.

No time to cook in the morning? Simply place the grain and water in a slow cooker and let the porridge simmer all night long. Quickly steam some greens and you're on your way. If you prefer a sweet porridge for breakfast, simply cook some seasonal or dried fruit in with the grain for a sweet morning repast.

I season whole grains most often with sea salt and nothing else. A cooking trick I learned years ago is to bring the grain to a boil, uncovered. Add a pinch of salt per cup of grain, cover, and reduce the heat to low. Simmer until all the liquid has been absorbed and the grain is tender. The results are perfect every time.

I don't know about you, but I always seem to cook too much grain for one meal. Turns out, that's a good thing for us. Leftover grain can be sautéed with vegetables, rolled with nori into sushi, mixed together with lightly cooked vegetables and a drizzle of dressing for a salad, made into small spheres and fried into croquettes, pressed into loaves, or used as flourless pie crusts . . . the possibilities are limited only by what you can imagine.

Whole grains nourish us on so many levels energetically. For example, rice is governed by the transformation of Metal, while millet is nourished by Earth, quinoa and corn by Fire, barley and oats by Tree, and kasha by Water. Varying your grains results in overall balance in your body.

And you thought eating whole grains meant a pile of rice on your plate every day for the rest of your life.

SPICY RICE WITH BABY LENTILS AND CANDIED ONIONS

Combining the stamina of brown rice with the peppery vitality provided by lentils will give you a splendid, rooted energy that allows you to lighten up and keep your options open.

Makes 3 to 4 servings

1 tablespoon avocado oil

2 to 3 red onions, cut into thin half-moons

Dash organic soy sauce, plus more to taste

1 (1-inch) piece kombu or 1 bay leaf

½ cup dried du Puy or black lentils, sorted and rinsed well

3½ cups spring or filtered water, divided

1 bay leaf

2 whole allspice

1 cinnamon stick

1 cup brown basmati rice, rinsed well

Pinch sea salt

Small handful fresh flatleaf parsley, minced, for garnish

Heat the avocado oil in a skillet over medium heat and cook the onions with a splash of soy sauce until they are quite limp and lightly browned, 15 to 20 minutes, stirring frequently.

While the onions cook, place the kombu (or bay leaf) in a heavy pot. Top with the lentils and add 1½ cups of the water. Bring to a boil, uncovered. Cover, reduce the heat to low, and cook until the lentils are tender, about 45 minutes. Season to taste with soy sauce and simmer, uncovered, for 5 to 7 minutes more, allowing any remaining liquid to be absorbed into the beans. Remove and discard the kombu (or bay leaf).

While the lentils simmer, cook the rice: Bring the remaining 2 cups water to a boil in a heavy pot, with the bay leaf, allspice, and cinnamon stick. Add the rice and sea salt; cover and bring to a boil. Reduce the heat to low and cook for 40 to 45 minutes, until all liquid has been absorbed. Remove from the heat, carefully remove the bay leaf, allspice, and cinnamon from the rice, and mound the rice in the center of a serving platter.

Combine the lentils with the candied onions and spoon this mixture around the rice. Garnish with parsley and serve immediately.

KASHA WITH NOODLES

Kasha keeps us feeling warm and strong, with lots of endurance. This simple main course is laced through with noodles and richly sautéed vegetables, making it deeply soul-satisfying as well as nourishing on chilly nights.

Makes 2 to 3 servings

2 teaspoons extra-virgin olive oil

½ red onion, diced

Sea salt

1 small carrot, diced

½ cup diced celery

1 cup fresh shiitake mushrooms, brushed free of dirt, thinly sliced

1 cup buckwheat groats (kasha), rinsed well and drained

1¼ cups spring or filtered water

Dash organic soy sauce

3 cups cooked noodles, such as mini shells, elbows, or bow ties

Small handful fresh flatleaf parsley, minced, for serving

Combine the olive oil and onion in a skillet over medium heat. When the onion begins to sizzle, add a pinch of salt and sauté until translucent, about 2 minutes. Add the carrot and celery with a pinch of salt and sauté for 1 to 2 minutes. Add the mushrooms with another pinch of salt, and sauté until the mushrooms release their juices into the skillet. Season lightly with salt. Cover, reduce the heat to low, and simmer for 7 to 10 minutes.

While the vegetables simmer, heat a dry skillet over medium heat. Dry roast the kasha, stirring constantly, until slightly darker and fragrant, about 2 minutes. Bring the water to a boil in a small pot. Stir in the toasted kasha and a dash of soy sauce. Cover, reduce the heat to low, and simmer for 15 to 20 minutes, until the buckwheat has absorbed all the cooking liquid.

Stir the cooked vegetables and noodles into the kasha and garnish with minced parsley. Serve warm.

HATO MUGI RISOTTO

This is brilliant—a creamy, rich, satisfying dish that helps the body assimilate oil, fat, and protein. This whole-grain dish improves kidney function and digestion and promotes healthy, glowing skin. Laced through with moisturizing vegetables, this barley dish is the perfect beauty treatment.

Makes 4 to 5 servings

DASHI

5 cups spring or filtered water
1 (3-inch) piece kombu
4 to 5 slices fresh ginger
1 dried shiitake mushroom
Dash organic soy sauce

RISOTTO

1 teaspoon extra-virgin olive oil
1 small yellow onion, diced
Sea salt
1 small carrot, diced
½ cup diced daikon
1 cup hato mugi barley, rinsed well
2 to 3 stalks broccoli, florets cut into tiny pieces, stems peeled and diced
2 tablespoons unsweetened almond or soy milk

To make the dashi: Combine the water, kombu, ginger, shiitake, and soy sauce in a pot and bring to a boil over medium-high heat. Reduce the heat to low and simmer for 15 minutes. Remove the ginger, shiitake, and kombu with a slotted spoon. The dashi will continue to simmer throughout the risotto cooking process, so keep the heat very low.

To make the risotto: Heat the olive oil and onion in a skillet over medium heat. When the onion begins to sizzle, add a pinch of salt and sauté until translucent, about 2 minutes. Add the carrot, daikon, and a pinch of salt and sauté until shiny with oil. Add the barley and sauté for 1 minute. Add the dashi to the barley in ½-cup quantities, stirring frequently. Add more dashi only as the previous ½ cup has been absorbed into the grain. The barley will cook for about 30 minutes, turning creamy as you slowly add the dashi, but will still hold its shape.

While the barley cooks, bring a pot of water to a boil and blanch the broccoli stems and florets until crisp-tender and bright green, about 1 minute. Drain and set aside.

When the risotto is ready, stir in the milk and reserved broccoli. Transfer to a serving bowl and serve immediately.

COOK'S TIP: *Hato mugi barley, also known as Job's tears, dates back to biblical times and is actually a Japanese grass seed used in Japanese Kampo (traditional herbal medicine) for treating bronchitis and other respiratory ailments. This amazing grain is also traditionally used in Asian cultures for weight loss and beauty, either made into teas or used externally as a facial mask.*

Hato mugi is often sold under the name "pearl barley," but should not be confused with pearled barley, which is regular barley that has been partially milled. It can be found in many natural foods stores, Asian markets, or online from companies selling macrobiotic supplies.

CRANBERRY-PECAN BREAD WITH CARAWAY SEEDS

This variation on a traditional New England bread is laced through with tart cranberries, richly toasted pecans, and savory caraway seeds. I like to serve this delicately sweet and spicy bread on a crisp autumn morning with a drizzle of brown rice syrup that I've seasoned with grated orange zest.

Makes 8 to 10 servings

3 ounces unsweetened dried cranberries

½ cup fresh orange juice

2 cups whole wheat pastry or sprouted whole wheat flour

½ cup organic yellow cornmeal

3 tablespoons coconut sugar

2 teaspoons baking powder

1 teaspoon baking soda

1 teaspoon caraway seeds

¼ teaspoon sea salt

¼ cup avocado oil

⅓ cup Suzanne's Specialties brown rice syrup

2 teaspoons pure vanilla extract

2 teaspoons grated orange zest

1½ cups unsweetened almond, rice, or soy milk

½ cup pecan pieces, lightly toasted

Preheat the oven to 350°F and lightly oil and flour a 10-inch deep-dish pie plate.

Mix the dried cranberries and orange juice together in a small bowl and soak them for about 15 minutes, stirring occasionally. Drain, discarding any excess juice.

Whisk together the flour, cornmeal, coconut sugar, baking powder, baking soda, caraway seeds, and salt in a mixing bowl. Mix in the avocado oil, brown rice syrup, vanilla extract, and orange zest. Slowly add the milk until you achieve a thick, spoonable batter. Do not overmix. Fold in the pecans and cranberries.

Spoon the batter evenly into the prepared pie plate and bake for about 35 minutes, until the center of the bread springs back to the touch or a toothpick inserted comes out clean. Cool for about 10 minutes, then run a sharp knife around the rim and slice the bread into wedges. Serve warm or at room temperature. This bread will keep for 3 to 4 days, tightly wrapped or in a sealed container at room temperature. It also freezes quite well.

TOFU-VEGETABLE ROLLS

This lovely starter course or light lunch provides you with lots of protein and complex carbs to give you staying power. We think of nori rolls as intimidating, but the method is so easy, you'll find yourself making these all the time.

Makes 3 to 4 servings

BAKED TOFU

2 (¼-inch-thick) slices
 extra-firm tofu, each cut
 into 4 spears
1 tablespoon organic
 soy sauce
1 tablespoon light sesame oil
1 (2-inch) piece fresh
 ginger, juice extracted,
 pulp discarded (see
 Cook's Tip, page 54)

RICE

1½ cups short-grain brown
 rice, rinsed well
3 cups spring or filtered
 water
3 pinches sea salt

ROLLS

½ cup shredded red
 cabbage
Dash red wine vinegar
3 sheets toasted nori
Stone-ground mustard,
 to taste
3 thin cucumber spears,
 cut the same length as
 the nori

To make the tofu: In a shallow bowl, cover the tofu spears with spring or filtered water. Add the soy sauce and sesame oil, followed by the ginger juice. Allow the tofu to marinate for 10 minutes.

Preheat the oven to 400°F. Drain the tofu, reserving the marinade, and spread the tofu spears on an unlined baking sheet. Bake for 30 to 35 minutes, uncovered, until browned, turning once midway through cooking to ensure even browning. Set aside.

To make the rice: Combine the rice and water in a heavy pot. Cover loosely and bring to a boil. Add the salt and reduce the heat to low. Cook until all the liquid has been absorbed, 30 to 40 minutes. Transfer the rice to a bowl and fluff with a rice paddle or wooden spoon to keep it from clumping. Set aside to cool.

While the rice and tofu are cooking, make the rolls: Bring a pot of water to a boil and blanch the cabbage for 30 seconds to 1 minute. Drain well and toss the cabbage with a generous sprinkle of red wine vinegar. This will give the cabbage a delicate sour taste and a beautiful pink color. Set aside.

To assemble the sushi rolls, place a sheet of nori, shiny side down, on a bamboo sushi mat or tea towel. Press one-third of the cooked rice onto the nori, spreading evenly to cover, leaving 1 inch of nori exposed on the side furthest from you. On the edge of rice closest to you, spread a thin layer of mustard. Lay 3 tofu spears end to end to cover the width of the nori. Lay a cucumber spear next to the tofu, and on top of that a narrow row of cabbage.

Using the mat as a guide, roll the nori around the rice and filling, pressing gently as you roll, creating a firm, filled »

>> cylinder. Moisten the exposed nori edge with water and seal the roll shut. Lay the roll on a dry surface, seam side down. Moisten the blade of a wet knife and slice the roll into 8 equal pieces. Repeat with the balance of ingredients to create 3 rolls. Arrange the pieces, cut side up, on a platter. Serve with the tofu marinade on the side as a dipping sauce.

COOK'S TIP: *You can purchase packaged baked tofu in most natural food stores or supermarkets, so you can save this step in the recipe process when you're in a hurry.*

BROWN RICE AND MILLET CROQUETTES

These tasty croquettes are another way to get blood sugar–stabilizing millet into your diet, and a delicious way to use leftover whole grains to create a lovely side dish to any meal.

Makes 3 to 4 servings

½ cup leftover cooked brown rice
½ cup leftover cooked millet
2 tablespoons finely diced onion
2 tablespoons finely diced carrot
¼ cup organic corn kernels (fresh or frozen, optional)
Avocado oil, for shallow frying
Fine organic yellow cornmeal, for dredging

In a bowl, combine the brown rice, millet, onion, carrot, and corn (if using) until well incorporated. Begin warming a generous coating of oil in a deep skillet over medium-low heat. With moist hands, form the mixture into small spheres, thick disks, or oblong disks. Pour some cornmeal onto a plate and dredge each croquette thoroughly before frying. This will hold the croquette together as well as give it a crispy outer coating.

Fry each croquette until golden brown, turning once to ensure even browning, and drain well on parchment paper or paper towels to remove any excess oil.

COOK'S TIP: *Don't be limited to this combo. Any cooked whole or cracked grains will make delicious croquettes. Rice with bulgur, millet with couscous, or barley and corn—the list is virtually endless. Dressed up with some diced veggies worked through, these croquettes are almost a meal in themselves. I will say, though, that millet makes the best croquettes, as its natural creaminess binds them easily.*

FARRO WITH CAULIFLOWER

Farro may be my favorite grain—it cooks quickly and goes with any meal. Rich in fiber and complex B vitamins, with more protein than wheat, this ancient grain with a low-gluten content can be traced back to 5000 BCE.

Makes 3 to 4 servings

- 2 teaspoons extra-virgin olive oil
- ½ red onion, diced
- 2 garlic cloves, minced
- Sea salt
- ¼ head cauliflower, broken into small florets
- Grated zest of ½ lemon
- 1 cup farro
- 2 cups spring or filtered water
- 2 to 3 sprigs fresh basil, leaves removed, coarsely chopped, for serving

Warm the oil, onion, and garlic in a medium saucepan over medium heat. When the onion begins to sizzle, add a pinch of salt and sauté for 2 to 3 minutes. Stir in the cauliflower and lemon zest. Add the farro and water and bring to a boil. Add a generous pinch of salt, cover, and reduce the heat to low. Cook until all the liquid has been absorbed and the farro is tender, 20 to 25 minutes. Stir in the fresh basil and serve warm or at room temperature.

COOK'S TIP: *While I rinse most whole grains, I don't usually rinse farro. You can if you like, but I find that it gets too soft when I rinse it. I do sort for any pebbles, but it's usually pretty clean.*

THANKSGIVING RICE

Holiday cooking doesn't mean that your health has to go down the tubes, especially if you serve this very special showstopper. Nutty brown rice, sweet corn, tart dried cranberries, and zesty citrus flavors all come together to create a special occasion dish that's worth celebrating.

Makes 4 to 5 servings

1 cup medium-grain brown rice, rinsed well

½ cup brown basmati rice, rinsed well

½ cup unsweetened dried cranberries, soaked in warm water for 15 minutes and drained

½ cup organic corn kernels (fresh or frozen)

Grated zest and juice of 1 lime

Grated zest and juice of 1 orange

3 cups spring or filtered water

Generous pinch sea salt

1 cup coarsely minced pecans

Combine the rices, cranberries, corn, lime zest, orange zest, and water in a heavy pot. Cover loosely and bring to a boil. Add the salt and cover. Reduce the heat to low and cook for 40 to 45 minutes, until all the liquid has been absorbed and the rice is fluffy.

While the rice cooks, place a dry skillet over medium heat. Pan toast the pecan pieces by stirring them in the hot skillet until lightly browned and fragrant, taking care not to burn them. Transfer to a small bowl to cool.

When the rice is cooked, gently fold in the toasted nuts, lime juice, and orange juice. Transfer to a serving bowl and serve immediately.

SWEET CORN FRITTERS

These fried corn fritters are the perfect starter or summer party food. The sweet taste of corn, along with its sunny summer vitality, combines with the strong sprouting energy of scallions to keep it light and fresh.

Makes 6 to 8 servings

½ cup whole wheat pastry or sprouted whole wheat flour

¼ cup organic yellow cornmeal

1 teaspoon baking powder

½ teaspoon powdered ginger

Generous pinch sea salt

3 to 4 ounces soft tofu, crumbled

Juice of ½ lemon

½ to ⅔ cup unsweetened almond, soy, or rice milk

1 cup organic corn kernels (fresh or frozen)

4 to 5 fresh scallions, diced

Small handful fresh flatleaf parsley, minced

Avocado oil, for frying

Preheat the oven to 275°F.

Combine the flour, cornmeal, baking powder, ginger, and sea salt in a bowl. Mix in the tofu and lemon juice. Slowly add the milk and mix to form a thick, smooth batter. Fold in the corn, scallions, and parsley, combining well.

Heat enough oil to coat the bottom of a skillet over medium heat. Drop the batter by tablespoons into the hot oil and cook for 3 to 4 minutes on each side, turning once, until the fritters are golden and crispy. Drain on parchment paper or paper towels, then transfer to the oven to keep warm. Repeat with the remaining batter, adding oil to the skillet as needed. Serve immediately.

COOK'S TIP: *These go especially well with a spicy dipping sauce, like soy sauce, water, and wasabi, or a Chinese-style plum sauce.*

MILLET WITH SWEET VEGETABLES AND CORN

We all love comfort food; it makes us feel so nurtured and satisfied. Nurturing is millet's special calling. In this recipe, millet and sweet vegetables combine to create a wonderfully relaxed energy, nourishing our middle organs—the organs that govern how well we manage stress in our lives—the spleen, stomach, and pancreas.

Makes 3 to 4 servings

¼ cup minced yellow onion
¼ cup minced winter squash
¼ cup minced carrot
½ cup organic corn kernels (fresh or frozen)
1 cup yellow millet, rinsed well
5 cups spring or filtered water
Pinch sea salt
Small handful pumpkin seeds, pan toasted, for serving

Layer the onion, squash, carrot, corn, and then millet in a heavy pot. Gently add the water, then cover and bring to a boil over medium heat. Add the salt, cover, and reduce the heat to low. Simmer until all the liquid has been absorbed into the millet and the grain is creamy, 25 to 30 minutes. Stir gently to combine the ingredients and transfer to a serving bowl. Serve immediately, garnished with freshly toasted pumpkin seeds.

MINTED QUINOA WITH CRUNCHY PINE NUTS

Quinoa is the perfect grain for those with an active lifestyle, but even those who are more sedentary can benefit from its energy-boosting qualities. It's nutritious, high in protein, and quick cooking, with an appealing nutty flavor. Quinoa needs to be rinsed very well to remove the oily saponin that coats the grain, or it will have an unpleasant, bitter flavor.

Makes 3 to 4 servings

1 cup quinoa, rinsed very well
1 cup tiny cauliflower florets
2 cups spring or filtered water
Dash organic soy sauce
½ cup pine nuts, pan toasted until golden brown
2 to 3 fresh scallions, thinly sliced on the diagonal
Small handful fresh mint, minced

Combine the quinoa, cauliflower, and water in a saucepan. Bring to a boil, then season with a splash of soy sauce, cover, and reduce the heat to low. Simmer until all the liquid has been absorbed and the quinoa has opened up, about 17 minutes. Gently fold in the pine nuts, scallions, and mint, then transfer to a serving bowl and serve immediately.

COOK'S TIP: *To pan toast pine nuts, warm a stainless steel skillet over medium heat. Toast the nuts, stirring constantly, until lightly browned and fragrant, about 3 minutes. Do not walk away when toasting pine nuts as they burn easily.*

ITALIAN COUSCOUS AND VEGGIE SALAD

There's nothing quite like a quick-cooking, light grain dish to cool the body in warm weather. Using couscous as a neutral foundation, we pull together olives, sun-dried tomatoes, fresh herbs, and bitter greens to create incredible energy. With the staying power you get from tempeh added to the mix, this dish will have you playing volleyball in the yard well after everyone else has tired out.

Makes 3 to 4 servings

1 cup spring or
   filtered water
Sea salt
1 cup couscous
2 to 3 teaspoons
   extra-virgin olive oil
1 small red onion, diced
2 garlic cloves, finely minced
2 to 3 tablespoons capers,
   drained
8 to 10 oil-cured black
   olives, pitted and diced
6 to 8 sun-dried tomatoes,
   soaked in water
   until tender, drained,
   and diced
1 small bunch baby arugula
3 to 4 sprigs fresh basil,
   leaves coarsely
   chopped, plus several
   whole sprigs for serving
4 ounces tempeh,
   crumbled, sautéed
   until golden brown
   (see Cook's Tip)

Bring the water to a boil in a saucepan with a pinch of sea salt. Add the couscous, cover, and turn off the heat. Allow to stand, undisturbed, for 5 minutes. Fluff with a fork and set aside.

Combine the olive oil, onion, and garlic in a skillet over medium heat. When the onion begins to sizzle, add a pinch of salt and sauté until translucent, about 2 minutes. Stir in the capers, followed by the olives and sun-dried tomatoes. Reduce the heat to low and cook, stirring occasionally, until the tomatoes are soft, 5 to 7 minutes. Turn off the heat and stir in the arugula, basil, and a light sprinkle of salt. Stir well to combine.

To serve, gently stir the cooked veggies and tempeh into the couscous. Serve immediately, garnished with fresh basil sprigs.

COOK'S TIP: *To brown tempeh, heat a small amount of oil in a skillet and add crumbled tempeh. Sprinkle with sea salt or a splash of soy sauce and cook, stirring constantly, until golden and slightly crispy, 4 to 5 minutes.*

TEMPURA VEGETABLES OVER SOBA NOODLES IN BROTH

This is vitality in a one-dish meal. The combination of strengthening buckwheat noodles with the richness of batter-fried root and sweet vegetables works within a savory, gingered broth to create a strong body and clear mind. All that and it tastes great!

Makes 3 to 4 servings

DASHI

- 4 cups spring or filtered water
- ¼ cup organic soy sauce
- 1 (1-inch) piece kombu
- 1 to 2 dried shiitake mushrooms, soaked in water until soft, stemmed
- 5 to 6 slices fresh ginger

TEMPURA BATTER

- 1 cup whole wheat pastry or sprouted whole wheat flour
- Pinch sea salt
- 1 tablespoon kuzu root, dissolved in a small amount of cold water
- ¾ to 1 cup dark beer or sparkling water

NOODLES AND VEGETABLES

- 8 ounces soba noodles
- 1 onion, sliced into thin rings
- 1 to 2 carrots, cut into thin oblong slices
- 1 medium burdock root, cut into thin oblong slices
- 1 small sweet potato, cut into thin oblong slices
- Handful cremini mushrooms, brushed free of dirt, halved
- 2 stalks broccoli, cut into small florets
- 2 quarts avocado or non-GMO sunflower oil, for frying
- 2 to 3 fresh scallions, thinly sliced on the diagonal, for serving

To make the dashi: Combine the water, soy sauce, kombu, shiitakes, and ginger in a pot. Bring to a boil, covered. Reduce the heat to low and remove the kombu, shiitakes, and ginger. Slice the shiitakes and kombu into thin pieces and return them to the broth. Discard the ginger. Simmer for 15 to 20 minutes, covered, to develop the flavors.

To make the tempura batter: Combine the flour and salt in a bowl. Stir in the dissolved kuzu root. Slowly add the beer or sparkling water to form a thin, spoonable batter, taking care that it's not too runny. Set the batter aside for 10 minutes before using. The sparkling water or beer and the kuzu are what will make your coating crispy, so they are important ingredients.

To make the noodles and vegetables: Bring a large pot of salted water to a boil and cook noodles according to package directions until al dente. Drain and rinse well. Set the noodles aside in the colander while you cook the vegetables, as they will need a quick rinse to loosen them before serving.

Spread the vegetables on a platter for easy access and place the bowl of tempura batter next to them. Heat about 3 inches of oil in a deep pot over medium heat. To make sure the oil is hot enough to start frying, submerge a pair of chopsticks in the oil. If bubbles accumulate around the chopsticks, the oil is ready. Raise the heat to high and, working in batches, begin dipping the vegetables into the tempura batter and dropping them gently into the oil. Fry until crispy and golden brown. The average frying time is 1 to 2 minutes—try not to leave the vegetables in the oil too long or they will be oily instead of crispy. Drain well on »

» parchment paper or paper towels. Repeat with the remaining ingredients. You may want to keep the fried veggies in a warm oven (200°F) to keep them crisp while you continue to work.

To assemble, rinse the noodles quickly and mound in individual serving bowls. Ladle the broth over the noodles and top generously with the tempura veggies. Serve immediately, garnished with fresh scallions.

COOK'S TIP: *It's important to use kuzu root (kudzu) in this recipe and not arrowroot powder, as it is a key ingredient in creating the crisp texture you are looking for in tempura-style cooking.*

SESAME NOODLE SALAD

Spicy sauces mixed in with mild noodles give abundant energy and clarity of thought. The noodles relax us, while the spices stimulate our thinking and inspire us to action. Be sure to rinse the somen noodles well, as Japanese noodles are coated with salt and require rinsing for the best flavor.

Makes 3 to 4 servings

1 pound somen noodles
¼ cup toasted sesame oil
1 (1-inch) piece fresh ginger, juice extracted, pulp discarded (see Cook's Tip, page 54)
¼ cup sesame tahini
2 teaspoons organic soy sauce
1 teaspoon chili powder
1 tablespoon brown rice vinegar, plus more to taste
6 to 8 fresh scallions, thinly sliced on the diagonal, for serving
3 to 4 tablespoons black sesame seeds, lightly pan toasted, for serving

Bring a large pot of water to a boil and cook the noodles according to package directions until al dente, 6 to 8 minutes. Drain and rinse well with cold water.

While the noodles cook, heat the sesame oil in a skillet over very low heat. Stir in the ginger juice and cook for 1 to 2 minutes to "open" the flavor. Remove from the heat and whisk in the tahini, soy sauce, and chili powder. Whisk in the rice vinegar to taste. Adjust the seasoning to your liking.

To serve, simply toss the cooked noodles with the sauce and scallions and transfer to a serving platter. Garnish with the black sesame seeds. Serve at room temperature or chilled.

COOK'S TIP: *If you are serving this dish chilled, do not mix the sauce into the pasta until just before you are ready to serve, as it can thicken and become pasty. Chill the sauce and the noodles separately. Rinse the cold noodles and mix together with the sauce.*

If you make the dressing ahead, you may need to add a small amount of water to thin it when ready to mix into the noodles.

SOBA NOODLES WITH CRISPY SEITAN AND VEGETABLES

This one-dish meal combines delicious flavor with tremendous energy. Soba noodles made from strengthening buckwheat provide enduring stamina. The rich protein of fried seitan gives us great stamina, and just so things don't get too heavy, there are loads of lightly cooked veggies for freshness.

Makes 3 to 4 servings

8 ounces soba noodles
1 cup organic corn kernels (fresh or frozen)
Handful snow peas, trimmed and left whole
1 to 2 carrots, julienned
2 stalks broccoli, cut into small florets, stems peeled and thinly sliced
2 to 3 fresh shiitake mushrooms, stemmed and thinly sliced
1 ripe pear, halved, cored, and thinly sliced
Juice of 1 lemon
Organic soy sauce, to taste
1 teaspoon kuzu root or arrowroot powder, dissolved in a small amount of cold water
Avocado or non-GMO sunflower oil, for frying
1 cup whole wheat pastry flour
Small handful sesame seeds, lightly pan toasted
8 ounces seitan, thickly sliced
2 to 3 fresh scallions, thinly sliced on the diagonal, for serving

Bring a large pot of salted water to a boil and cook the noodles according to package directions until al dente. Drain and rinse well to remove the extra salt that coats the noodles.

While the noodles cook, bring a small pot of salted water to a boil and begin cooking the vegetables separately, in the order listed above, beginning with the corn kernels and ending with the shiitakes. You want them to be just crisp-tender, so don't boil them to death. The shiitakes will take a bit longer than the rest of the vegetables, so test them.

Combine the veggies in a large mixing bowl. Toss the pear with the lemon juice and mix it in with veggies, juice and all. Transfer 1 cup of the vegetable cooking water to another small pot. Warm through over low heat. Season lightly with soy sauce and stir in the dissolved kuzu, stirring until the mixture thickens. Spoon the mixture over the cooked vegetables and mix well to coat.

While cooking the noodles and veggies, heat about 1 inch of oil in a deep skillet. Combine the flour and sesame seeds in a shallow plate. Dredge the seitan slices in the mixture to coat well. When the oil is hot, fry the seitan until golden on both sides, turning to fry evenly. Drain well on parchment or paper towels.

To serve, toss the cooked noodles with the glazed veggie mixture and arrange on a serving platter. Top with the seitan and garnish with the scallion slices. Serve immediately.

PIADINE

Traditional Italian flatbreads are one of the many, many joys of Italian cooking. They are delicious and tender . . . and if they were any easier to make, they would make themselves. You will love these as wraps, with hummus, or sliced in half for a thin, panini-style sandwich.

Makes four 10-inch breads

8 ounces whole wheat
    bread flour
8 ounces durum flour,
    plus extra for dusting
    work surface
2 teaspoons sea salt
1 tablespoon baking powder
¼ cup extra-virgin olive oil
½ cup spring or
    filtered water

Combine the whole wheat flour, durum flour, salt, and baking powder in a large mixing bowl and mix well. Stir in the oil and water to form a soft dough. On a dry, lightly floured work surface, knead the dough for 10 minutes, until smooth and elastic. Divide into 4 pieces and roll each piece into a 10-inch, very thin round.

Heat a cast-iron skillet over medium heat and lay a piadina in the hot, dry pan. Cook for 3 to 4 minutes, or until the bread is lightly browned and beginning to blister. Flip the piadina and cook for 1 to 2 minutes more, or until the other side browns and blisters. Repeat with the remaining dough. Serve warm.

COOK'S TIP: *To make the dough ahead, just wrap in plastic and refrigerate for 2 to 3 days before use. Allow to come to room temperature before rolling.*

COOK'S TIP: *Durum is a type of wheat often used to make pasta. If the label says "100 percent whole wheat" or "100 percent whole durum flour," then you are getting the whole grain—bran, endosperm, and germ. King Arthur's White Whole Wheat Flour is a good choice.*

FABULOUS ENGLISH MUFFINS

Did you ever imagine you could easily make your own English muffins, complete with nooks and crannies? Well, you can. The flavor and texture of homemade English muffins is far superior to store-bought. One bite, and you'll be hooked!

Makes 10 to 12 muffins

1 teaspoon brown rice syrup or coconut sugar

1½ cups warm spring or filtered water, divided

2½ teaspoons (1 packet) active dry yeast

3 tablespoons extra-virgin olive oil

3 cups whole wheat pastry or sprouted whole wheat flour, plus more for kneading

2 teaspoons sea salt

In a large mixing bowl, stir the brown rice syrup (or coconut sugar) into ½ cup of the warm water until completely dissolved. Sprinkle the yeast over the surface of the water and set aside to stand until it bubbles, 5 to 7 minutes. Stir in the oil along with the remaining 1 cup warm water.

In another bowl, combine the flour and sea salt and mix well.

There are two ways to make and knead the dough: with a stand mixer or by hand.

Stand mixer: Attach the dough hook to the mixer. Place all but 1 cup of the flour in the mixer and turn speed to "2." Slowly add the yeast/water mixture until all the ingredients are combined and a soft dough forms. Slowly add the reserved 1 cup flour until a ball of dough forms and pulls away from the sides of the bowl. Continue to process at speed "2" to knead the dough for 7 minutes, adding small amounts of flour as needed so the ball of dough continues to clean the sides of the bowl and creates a soft ball.

By hand: Place all of the flour in a large, wide mixing bowl and form a well in the middle. Pour the yeast/water mixture into the well and begin mixing with a fork to pull the flour into the liquid. Once the dough forms a ball, knead by hand for 8 to 9 minutes, in the bowl, adding small amounts of flour as needed to create a soft ball of dough.

Once the dough has been kneaded in your stand mixer or by hand, proceed as follows:

Lightly oil a bowl that is twice as large as the dough. Transfer the dough to the oiled bowl and lightly turn it to coat with the oil. Cover tightly with plastic wrap, then cover the bowl with a light dish towel. Set aside in a warm place for 1½ to 2 hours, or until the dough doubles in size.

Once the dough has risen, turn it onto a lightly floured surface and knead 1 to 3 times.

Heat a lightly oiled large cast-iron skillet over medium heat.

Break the dough into balls about 2 inches in diameter. Place 4 to 6 dough balls on the surface of the hot skillet and press them down gently with a spatula, but do not flatten them completely. Think English muffin thickness. Allow to cook, undisturbed, for 4 minutes, lightly pressing the muffins every few minutes. The muffins will swell and increase in size by about 50 percent, so don't crowd the skillet.

After 4 minutes, flip the muffins and cook for another 4 minutes. You'll know the muffins are done when both sides have the typical browning you associate with English muffins. They will sound hollow when you tap on them.

Split with a fork before toasting and enjoy!

COOK'S TIP: *Wrapped tightly, the English muffins will keep, refrigerated, for about a week, or you can wrap and freeze them for as long as 3 months.*

PASTA WITH BROCCOLI-PINE NUT PESTO

We're all familiar with what we consider to be the classic pesto—fresh basil, pine nuts, olive oil, and garlic—but did you know that in Italian, *pesto* simply means "paste"? In Italian cuisine, pesto is made from just about any vegetable you can imagine. This one will win you raves. Richly flavored and brightly colored, with a creamy texture, this pesto smothers pasta with delicious flavor and disease-fighting antioxidants.

Makes 4 to 5 servings

2 stalks broccoli, cut into small florets, stems peeled and diced
1 pound fettuccine
½ cup pine nuts
½ cup walnut pieces
2 garlic cloves, smashed
3 to 4 tablespoons extra-virgin olive oil
1 tablespoon red wine vinegar
1 teaspoon brown rice syrup
1 tablespoon white miso
1 red bell pepper, roasted over an open flame, peeled, seeded, and diced (see Cook's Tip, page 113), for serving

Bring a large pot of water to a boil and cook the broccoli florets and stems until bright green and tender, about 3 minutes. Remove with a mesh strainer and set aside. In the same water, cook the pasta according to package directions until al dente, 8 to 10 minutes. Drain well, but do not rinse.

While the pasta cooks, lightly pan toast the pine nuts and walnuts until fragrant, about 2 minutes. Place the nuts in a food processor fitted with a metal blade along with the garlic, olive oil, vinegar, brown rice syrup, and miso. Puree until smooth. Add the broccoli and puree until a smooth, thick paste forms. If the pesto is too thick for your taste, add hot water a tablespoon at a time, but do not thin it too much or it will not cling to the pasta.

To serve, toss the hot fettuccine with the pesto and transfer to a serving platter. Serve immediately, garnished with the diced roasted pepper.

COOK'S TIP: *When buying dried pastas, look for those made with durum and/or semolina flours, as these are the least refined of Italian pasta flours. I would skip any white flour pasta, as it compromises digestion. With durum and semolina (both from light-colored wheat), you have some fiber left intact.*

FEAR AND LOATHING IN THE KITCHEN
HOW SOY AND GLUTEN BECAME DEMONS AND WHY THEY SHOULDN'T BE

I hear it in every cooking class. People are in real distress over gluten and soy products. So-called experts are warning us off both, en masse, but should we be avoiding these ancient foods that have nourished humans for thousands of years?

SOY VEY

We have been told that soy causes everything from thyroid conditions to undeveloped brains in infants. And then there's the impact on men: that they will lose their libidos, vitality, and grow breasts. Most women are terrified of their bodies having too much estrogen, and many doctors advise them to avoid tofu and soy products as they can cause an increased uptake of estrogen in the body.

Let's clear this right up. First, real men do eat tofu and because it contains lots of protein and no saturated fats, circulation remains strong, so men are less likely to face erectile dysfunction. As for our brains, a study conducted at the University of North Carolina, done only on mice, proved inconclusive. It was based on feeding the mice excessive estrogen, more than any human would consume, which in my humble opinion sort of negates the findings.

However, the topic most worrisome for us with soy: cancer.

A recent study reported by MD Anderson Cancer Centers concluded that traditional soy products were not only linked to reduced risk of breast cancer, but an actual benefit to survivors in prevention of recurrence, not to mention overall longevity, with or without cancer.

The study reports that the American Cancer Society revealed that "when it comes to soy, isoflavones may act like estrogen, but they have anti-estrogen properties as well" with some studies showing that women who eat soy are less likely to develop breast cancer.

According to the National Institute of Health (NIH), "Increased levels of estrogen metabolites (EM) are associated with cancers of the reproductive system. One potential dietary source of EM is milk. In this study, the absolute quantities of unconjugated (free) and unconjugated plus conjugated (total) EM were measured in a variety of commercial milks (whole, 2%, skim, and buttermilk). The results

Fully mature beans can also be picked, cleaned, dried, and stored, and this is how we most commonly eat them. At this stage, they will need to be cooked for some time to become tender enough to digest.

But what about that . . . you know . . . problem of digestion? Beans, beans, the musical fruit, and all that? Beans contain natural protease inhibitors, which are the source of their strong immune defenses. Beans are tough and endure in most weather conditions as they grow and mature. These same elements can inhibit digestion. This is where cooking comes in, as heat breaks down the protease inhibitors. And don't forget to chew your beans. Chewing is most effective at rendering beans digestible.

The protein in beans is incredibly concentrated, great for building dense, solid muscle in our bodies. In fact, beans are higher in protein than most animal foods, only falling a bit short in the essential amino acid department, which we easily obtain from other foods.

Now that we have that out of the way, let's cook beans. Cooking beans is easy, but requires a small commitment of time. Some cooking experts insist on soaking beans for as long as overnight, but I have found that it's not usually necessary, although there are a couple of exceptions.

I was working in Italy many years ago in a small villa. The chef at the villa was an older Italian woman whose skill in the kitchen was mind-boggling. She created dishes from the simplest ingredients that stunned and delighted the guests. For this group, we took over her kitchen to cook for our guests, but she came to the kitchen every day to check up on us.

One day, I was draining the soaking water from beans and she asked me why I didn't like my guests. What? She said that I was throwing away the flavor of the beans along with people's ability to digest them. *What?* I explained that you soak beans to break down some of the indigestible sugars that give people gas. And, I added, the beans would cook more quickly. She waved her hand at me and said that I was also throwing away *enzimi*—enzymes. *What?*

Then she challenged me to cook beans alongside her; she would cook hers without soaking and I would cook mine as they were. It was like an episode of *Chopped*. Side by side, knife stroke matching knife stroke, we cooked, matching ingredients. In the end, her beans cooked a few minutes faster than mine, had incredible flavor, and no one, not one person, was "musical" after eating.

I haven't soaked a bean since, with one exception (see below). So stop soaking. Now. You'll thank me later.

Here's how I cook beans: Sort through them for small stones, and wash them very well to remove dust. Put them in a pan with three times the amount of water as beans, along with a bay leaf or 1-inch piece of kombu to help tenderize the indigestible sugars, fiber, and proteins, and bring to a boil, uncovered. Reduce the heat to low, cover, and cook until tender, usually about an hour. It's that easy. I often add large chunks of onion, carrot, and celery. I say large chunks because you'll be straining these off when the beans are tender. I also add a pinch of salt after the beans come to a boil. You're not seasoning the beans, just adding a pinch. I've found that a pinch ensures even tenderness throughout the pot of beans. I have no idea why, but it works; just be sure not to add too much salt or the beans won't cook to tenderness at all. Just a pinch.

My one exception to the "no soaking" rule is chickpeas. I learned this great trick in Israel and it only works on chickpeas. I have no idea why. Soak your chickpeas for one hour in cold water with a tablespoon of baking soda for every cup of chickpeas. After the hour, drain and rinse the beans very well. Proceed with cooking until tender.

The rule of thumb is simple. For bean dishes or stews, use three times the water to beans. For soups, use four to five times the water depending on how thick or thin you prefer your soups. I usually begin with four times the water and thin as I desire once the beans are softening.

Some people struggle mightily with cooking beans, saying that they take forever to soften or that some beans become tender and some not so much, resulting in a bizarre mix of overly hard and seriously mushy beans. If this is you, read on. Surely, the cause of this could be old beans. When dried beans become stale, they just refuse to cook properly. They're old and cranky. If the beans in your pantry are more than a year old: a) you really need to cook beans more and b) toss them and buy new beans. Even organic beans are affordable on most budgets, so splurge and buy fresh ones. And cook them.

What goes into a great bean dish? What do you like? Sure, there are traditions and flavors that you naturally think of, but once you've mastered those, go crazy. Cook your beans with the veggies and flavorings you love. These recipes are simply your jumping-off point to delicious bean feasts. I cook my beans simply. I sauté diced onion, celery, and carrot (a classic mirepoix or soffritto) in good olive oil and add to my beans once they're tender. You can sauté the veggies first, top with the beans and water, and cook until tender as well (and skip the cooking with chunks of veggies in that case) with great results. I often add crushed garlic to my sauté as well as fresh or canned diced tomatoes, depending on the season. I'll season to taste with sea salt and serve the beans with a generous drizzle of olive oil and a sprinkling of fresh herbs. It may sound plain to you, but if your veggies are fresh and your oil delicious, you'll find these bean dishes make the rest of the meal soar.

If you're feeling creative, switch up the vegetables. Cauliflower, onion, and garlic cooked in with the beans, with bitter greens stirred in, drizzled with olive oil just before serving, makes for a fine bean dish. Potatoes, finely diced and sautéed with your mirepoix, are divine with most beans. I always, always stir fresh herbs or delicate greens into a finished bean dish for color, freshness, and a light energy that balances the dish.

Hot spice, fresh lemon juice, certain spices like cumin, and fresh herbs like basil and rosemary turn simple bean dishes into feasts to be served with nothing more than great whole-grain bread and a crisp salad. You'll moan with pleasure over a meal like this; trust me. You can join the ranks of what Italians call *mangiafagioli* . . . bean eaters!

A few more things. Try to use organic beans when you can afford it, but don't let price or lack of access to organic products stop you from enjoying these nutrient-dense foods that are essential to good health and wellness.

Storing dried beans is easy. Keep beans in well-sealed glass jars with a dried bay leaf in each jar to keep them fresh. I use wide-mouth Mason-style jars and they work great. My beans are lined up in the pantry so I can see what I have and choose based on my tastes.

Keep some canned beans in the pantry for those late nights when you just can't eat tofu one more time, but try not to make canned beans a habit. They always taste stale to me, despite vigorous rinsing. But if they're what you must use, rinse them well before you add them to any recipe and be sure to use fresh ingredients in your dish to bring them back to life, so to speak.

I prefer to cook larger quantities of beans and freeze them in portioned containers. They thaw quickly and are so easy to use. Many are the nights that I sauté veggies, add a container of frozen beans and some water, and in 20 minutes we have a hearty, delicious soup. And in my house, there are always bread and salad ingredients, so we have a complete meal quickly.

Finally, not only do beans provide us with strength and stamina because they're rich sources of protein, but also, in terms of yin and yang and the theory we know as the Five Transformations of Energy, they're the greatest secret for staying big and strong. Most beans find themselves governed by Earth, Metal, and Water energies, all of which are strengthening and grounding, but in a very different way than protein from animals, which can make us feel tight, our muscles overly contracted. The energy in beans makes us strong and yet keeps the fluid grace we love in our muscles.

Plant-passionate proteins encompass more than beans, however. Traditional soy products like tofu, tempeh, and edamame and gluten-based seitan provide more options for protein in our diets. Quick to cook and versatile to use, these options provide not only protein but are also perfect when you're creating a traditional dish or trying to create a familiar feel to a dish as you transition to plant-passionate eating. Tofu can be used in Asian-inspired dishes, as it has for thousands of years, or used to create creamy sauces or a cheese-like consistency, and because it takes on the flavor of any seasoning, it has become the basis for many a "faux" dish. Tempeh has a firmer, meatier texture that lends itself to stews, casseroles, and sandwiches, and because it's fermented, many people find it a bit easier on digestion than tofu. They're both great and quite different, so you can mix and match to create the dishes you desire. Please choose organic when it comes to soy products, as we want to avoid GMO (genetically modified organism) foods until we know more definitive facts about them and their effects on human and planetary health.

Seitan is a unique product made from bread flour, which is kneaded in water to wash away the starch and fiber, leaving only the protein in wheat, called gluten. Cooked in a savory broth to create a meaty texture before it is packaged, seitan has a rich brown color and is used in any recipe as you would use chicken or beef.

The recipes here are made with basic ingredients found in most pantries because I find that the less fuss around beans and other proteins, the more flavorful they are. It's important to note that you can interchange the beans in every single recipe. If you don't like lentils (crazy as that sounds to me; I am obsessed with them . . .), you can use black, white, or brown beans. Play with your beans; find your favorites and enjoy them.

TEMPEH WITH LOTUS ROOT AND SAUERKRAUT

This perfect autumn stew is hearty and warming, yes, but that's not all. Tempeh, a fermented soy product, has a substantial texture and a warming energy in the body. The lotus root, a many-chambered tuber vegetable, is beneficial to our lung function, balancing moisture and increasing our breathing capacity. Fresh ginger, stewed onions, and cabbage warm and nourish the digestive tract to create a dish that will keep you toasty warm come winter.

Makes 3 to 4 servings

Avocado oil, for frying
8 ounces tempeh, cut into
   1-inch cubes
1 onion, cut into
   thick wedges
¼ head green cabbage,
   shredded
1 small lotus root, halved
   lengthwise, cut into
   ⅛-inch slices
½ cup natural sauerkraut,
   drained well, rinsed if
   too salty
1 (1-inch) piece fresh ginger,
   juice extracted, pulp
   discarded (see Cook's
   Tip, page 54)
Organic soy sauce, to taste
1 to 2 teaspoons kuzu root
   or arrowroot powder,
   dissolved in a small
   amount of cold water
Small handful fresh flatleaf
   parsley, minced,
   for serving

Generously cover the bottom of a deep skillet with the avocado oil and place over medium heat. When the oil is hot, panfry the tempeh until golden, turning once to evenly brown. Drain on paper towels and set aside.

Layer the onion, cabbage, lotus root, and fried tempeh in the same skillet. Add water to reach a depth of ¼ inch in the bottom of the skillet. Cover and bring to a boil over medium heat. Reduce the heat to low and simmer until the cabbage is quite limp, about 15 minutes. Add the sauerkraut and ginger juice and season lightly with soy sauce (considering the salt in the sauerkraut). Cover and simmer for 5 to 7 minutes more. Stir in the dissolved kuzu root to form a thin glaze over the stew. Transfer to a bowl and serve garnished with parsley.

COOK'S TIP: *You can use other vegetable oils for frying if you can't find or don't want to invest in avocado oil, but try to use the best quality your wallet allows. I suggest non-GMO sunflower or safflower oil if avocado is not an option.*

CROSTINI WITH LENTIL PÂTÉ

An earthy, peppery spread over toasted bread creates the perfect starter course that will keep you feeling grounded, with lots of endurance.

Makes 4 to 8 servings

2 teaspoons extra-virgin olive oil, plus more for brushing and drizzling

1 small red onion, finely diced

1 to 2 garlic cloves, smashed and minced

Sea salt

1 carrot, finely diced

1 stalk celery, finely diced

1 bay leaf

1 cup green or brown lentils, sorted and rinsed well

3 cups spring or filtered water

Dash balsamic vinegar

½ roasted red bell pepper, diced (see Cook's Tip, page 113)

1 whole-grain baguette, thickly sliced (½ to 1 inch)

Combine the oil, onion, and garlic in a saucepan over medium heat. When the onion begins to sizzle, add a pinch of salt and sauté until the onion is translucent, 2 to 3 minutes. Add the carrot and celery with a pinch of salt and sauté until shiny with oil. Spread the veggies over the bottom of the pot and add the bay leaf. Top with the lentils and water. Bring to a boil, uncovered. Cover, reduce the heat to low, and simmer until the lentils are quite soft, 35 to 40 minutes. Season to taste with salt and simmer for 3 to 5 minutes more. If any cooking liquid remains, remove the lid and cook over medium heat until the liquid is absorbed.

Remove from the heat, stir in a generous splash of balsamic vinegar, and transfer to a food processor. Puree, by pulsing, until thick and semi-smooth. You want a pâté-like texture, not a cream. Fold in the roasted red pepper.

To prepare the crostini, preheat the oven to 400°F. Place the bread on a baking sheet. Brush lightly with oil on the top side and sprinkle lightly with salt. Bake until golden and crispy, about 8 minutes. Set a timer so you don't burn the bread.

Spread the pâté on the warm, toasted bread and drizzle with olive oil. Serve immediately.

LENTIL WALDORF SALAD

In this delicious turn on a classic autumn salad, the earthy flavor of baby lentils is the perfect complement to the crisp apples and sweet pecans. But it isn't just another delicious salad—the lentils give us great endurance, the apples relax us, but with just enough tart flavor to give us some sparkle, and the pecans, like other nuts, grow into trees and so have lots of energy stored within. You'll be dancing in the streets.

Makes 3 to 4 servings

1 bay leaf
⅔ cup du Puy, Umbrian, or Beluga lentils, sorted and rinsed
1¼ cups spring or filtered water
Sea salt
2 to 3 Granny Smith apples, unpeeled, halved, cored, and diced, tossed in 1 teaspoon lemon juice
1 cup diced red onion, lightly blanched
2 stalks celery, diced
Grated zest of 1 lemon
½ cup walnut pieces, lightly toasted (see Cook's Tip)
¼ teaspoon nutmeg
⅔ cup vegan mayonnaise substitute

Place the bay leaf in a pot and top with the lentils and water. Bring to a boil, uncovered. Add a pinch of salt. Reduce the heat to low, cover, and cook until the lentils are tender but not too soft, about 35 minutes. Season lightly again with salt and simmer for 1 minute more. Drain and transfer to a small bowl to cool until just warm.

Prepare the salad by combining the cooked lentils with the apples, red onion, celery, lemon zest, walnuts, and nutmeg. Gently stir in the vegan mayo until the ingredients are well coated. Serve warm.

COOK'S TIP: *To toast walnut pieces, heat a dry stainless steel skillet over medium heat. Add the walnuts and cook, stirring constantly, until fragrant, about 3 minutes. Transfer to a bowl immediately to avoid burning.*

CANNELLINI BEANS WITH GREENS

Simple, elegant, and earthy, this classic Italian combination is warming and strengthening. It's easy to make, loaded with nutrients, and the greens add freshness and balance. Take your time simmering the beans so they cook to perfect al dente tenderness.

Makes 3 to 4 servings

2 teaspoons extra-virgin olive oil, plus more for drizzling
1 red onion, cut into small dice
2 garlic cloves, crushed
Sea salt
2 stalks celery, cut into small dice
1 medium carrot, cut into small dice
1 roasted red bell pepper, cut into small dice (see Cook's Tip, page 113)
½ cup cannellini beans, rinsed well (you can also use navy beans or any other white bean)
2 cups spring or filtered water
1 bay leaf
1 small bunch escarole, broccoli rabe, or kale, rinsed very well, hand shredded into bite-size pieces

In a deep skillet over medium heat, combine the olive oil, onion, and garlic. When the onion begins to sizzle, add a pinch of salt and sauté until translucent, about 3 minutes. Stir in the celery and a pinch of salt and sauté for 1 minute. Stir in the carrot and another pinch of salt and sauté for 1 minute more. Stir in the bell pepper and a pinch of salt and sauté for 1 minute. Add the beans, water, and bay leaf and bring to a boil. Add a final pinch of salt. Cover and reduce the heat to low. Cook until the beans are soft and all the water has been absorbed, about an hour. Remove the bay leaf.

Season with salt to your taste, but keep it light; stir in the greens and cook, covered, until they are tender and wilted, about 4 minutes. Stir well to combine and transfer to a serving bowl. Serve with a drizzle of fruity olive oil.

CANNELLINI PICCATA

You love chicken piccata, right? Think you can't live without it? You won't miss the bird once you have tasted this recipe. With no saturated fat or other nasty stuff we know comes in chicken, these spicy beans are satisfying, and studies show that eating cannellini beans once a week can help reduce the risk of heart disease. And with hot spice to stimulate circulation, this dish is a heart-healthy winner.

Makes 3 to 4 servings

2 tablespoons extra-virgin olive oil, plus more for drizzling

1 red onion, diced

3 garlic cloves, minced

Sea salt

Cracked black pepper, to taste

Crushed red pepper flakes, to taste

Grated zest of 1 lemon

10 cremini mushrooms, brushed free of dirt, coarsely chopped

2 tablespoons dry white wine

4 tablespoons whole wheat pastry flour

1½ cups spring or filtered water

2 cups cooked cannellini beans or 1 (15-ounce) can organic beans

3 to 4 sprigs fresh basil, leaves removed, coarsely chopped

2 to 3 sprigs fresh flatleaf parsley, coarsely chopped

Heat the olive oil, onion, and garlic in a deep skillet over medium heat. When the onion begins to sizzle, add a pinch of salt, a pinch of black pepper, and a generous pinch of red pepper flakes along with the lemon zest. Sauté for 2 to 3 minutes. Stir in the mushrooms and wine and sauté for 2 to 3 minutes.

Add the flour, stirring to coat the veggies, creating a smooth texture. Add the water and stir until thickened, about 3 minutes. Add the beans, another pinch of salt, plus a little more cracked pepper and red pepper flakes to taste. Cook over low heat, uncovered, stirring frequently, until bubbling and thick, about 5 minutes. Remove from the heat and stir in the basil and parsley. Serve over pasta or as a side dish, both with a generous drizzle of good olive oil.

CHICKPEAS WITH SAGE AND OLIVE OIL

If I could eat only one bean for the rest of my life, it would be chickpeas. Their silky texture lends sensual richness to any dish and then there's the fact that they can help protect our heart health. Could it get better? I think not.

Makes 2 to 3 servings

1 tablespoon extra-virgin olive oil, plus more for drizzling

½ red onion, cut into small dice

2 garlic cloves, crushed

½ teaspoon sea salt, plus more to taste

½ cup coarsely chopped fresh sage, plus 3 or 4 fresh leaves for serving

Scant pinch cracked black pepper

1 cup cooked chickpeas (see Cook's Tip)

¼ cup white wine

Juice of ½ lemon

Combine the olive oil, onion, and garlic in a skillet over medium heat. When the onion sizzles, add a pinch of salt and sauté until translucent, about 3 minutes. Add the chopped sage, pepper, chickpeas, wine, and ½ teaspoon salt. Reduce the heat to low and simmer until the beans are heated through and the wine has reduced a bit, 5 minutes. Remove from the heat and add the lemon juice. Stir well and serve garnished with fresh sage leaves and a generous drizzle of good olive oil.

COOK'S TIP: *You can use canned organic chickpeas in this recipe. Just rinse them well before use. Or you can cook ½ cup dried chickpeas, soaked for an hour with 2 teaspoons baking soda and then rinsed well, with 1½ cups water for about 1 hour. This will yield about 1 cup cooked chickpeas.*

CURRIED CHICKPEAS AND POTATOES

A quick and tasty main course, this will leave you with no excuses to order takeout. This spicy stew will satisfy you on many levels, so don't let the ingredients list intimidate you. It's lots of little pinches of spices and you can omit any that you wish and still have a great, nutrient-dense stew.

Makes 3 to 4 servings

1 tablespoon avocado or extra-virgin olive oil, plus more for drizzling
1 red onion, diced
3 garlic cloves, minced
1 teaspoon fresh minced ginger (from a 1-inch piece)
Sea salt
½ teaspoon ground cumin
½ teaspoon ground turmeric
¼ teaspoon crushed red pepper flakes
¼ teaspoon chipotle powder (or your favorite chili powder)
½ teaspoon curry powder
2 cups diced new or fingerling potatoes, left unpeeled
1 cup cooked chickpeas, rinsed well (or canned organic chickpeas; see Cook's Tip, page 187)
1 cup spring or filtered water
Juice of ½ lemon, plus more to taste
2 to 3 kale leaves (or other dark leafy green), coarsely chopped

Heat the oil in a deep skillet over medium heat. Add the onion, garlic, and ginger and a pinch of salt. Sauté for 2 minutes. Stir in the cumin, turmeric, crushed red pepper flakes, chipotle powder, and curry powder and mix well to coat the onion.

Add the potatoes and cook, stirring, until the potatoes are browned at the edges and tender, about 6 minutes. Add the chickpeas and water. Season with a pinch of salt. Bring to a boil, cover, and reduce the heat to low. Cook until all the liquid has been absorbed, 7 to 10 minutes. Remove from the heat and add the lemon juice and kale. Stir just until the kale is wilted, then season to taste with salt and more lemon juice. Serve with a generous drizzle of fruity olive oil.

KALE SALAD WITH CHICKPEAS

Need a lighter meal that's packed with protein? Here you go! Serve it with whole-grain bread and you are all set!

Makes 3 to 4 servings

1 bunch kale (lacinato
    or curly)
2 teaspoons plus
    3 tablespoons extra-
    virgin olive oil, divided
5 to 6 oil-cured sun-dried
    tomatoes, diced
¾ cup coarse bread crumbs
    (regular or gluten-free)
1 garlic clove, mashed
½ teaspoon sea salt
⅛ teaspoon cracked
    black pepper
Pinch crushed red
    pepper flakes
Juice of ½ lemon
1 cup cooked chickpeas,
    rinsed well (or canned
    organic chickpeas; see
    Cook's Tip, page 187)

Rinse the kale leaves and towel dry. Shred the kale leaves, removing the stems if they are thick. Dice the stems separately.

Heat 2 teaspoons of the olive oil in a skillet over medium heat. Sauté the sun-dried tomatoes and bread crumbs until the bread crumbs are golden brown, about 3 minutes. Set aside.

Mix together the garlic, salt, cracked pepper, crushed red pepper, the remaining 3 tablespoons olive oil, and the lemon juice. Adjust the seasonings to your taste and mix well.

Toss the kale and kale stems with the chickpeas, bread crumbs, and dressing to coat. Allow to marinate for about 15 minutes before serving.

COOK'S TIP: *You can also make a quick tahini dressing for this salad instead of the olive oil version. Mix together 3 to 4 tablespoons tahini with lemon juice, sea salt, and enough water to create your desired texture. Eliminate the red pepper flakes and olive oil.*

BLACK BEAN TACOS

Tacos and parties are the perfect pairing. It's so much fun to create a "build your own taco" station on your buffet, so people can pick and choose their favorite toppings. Vegan or not, everyone will love these tacos.

Makes 5 to 6 servings

1 tablespoon extra-virgin olive oil
1 small red onion, diced
2 to 3 garlic cloves, minced
Sea salt
1 serrano chile, seeded and minced
¼ teaspoon chili powder
1 carrot, diced
1 to 2 cups cremini mushrooms, brushed clean and thinly sliced
1 cup dried black turtle beans, sorted and rinsed
1 cup canned diced tomatoes
2½ cups spring or filtered water
Shredded romaine lettuce, for serving
Diced fresh tomatoes, for serving
Shredded vegan cheese substitute, cheddar or Monterey Jack flavor, for serving
10 to 12 chapati breads, lightly steamed, or hard or soft taco shells, for serving

Heat the olive oil, onion, and garlic in a deep skillet over medium heat. When the onion begins to sizzle, add a pinch of salt, the serrano chile, and the chili powder and sauté until the onion is translucent, about 2 minutes. Add the carrot and mushrooms and sauté for 1 minute.

Add the beans, tomatoes, water, and a pinch of salt. Cover and bring to a boil. Reduce the heat to low and cook until the beans are soft, about 1 hour. Season to taste with salt and simmer for 5 minutes more.

To serve, transfer the beans to a large bowl and arrange the toppings in small bowls with chapati or taco shells.

BLACK BEAN BURGERS

Bean burgers can be completely satisfying and delicious, even for people who love a meaty burger. They are so hearty and substantial that no one really misses the meat. I especially love this one because of the wee bit of spice that livens it up, and the fresh greens that add lightness and nutrition.

Makes 4 to 5 servings

BURGERS

½ cup diced red onion
½ cup whole wheat bread crumbs (or gluten-free bread crumbs)
¼ cup minced fresh basil
2 tablespoons minced jalapeño pepper
2 tablespoons vegan mayonnaise substitute (plus more for serving; optional)
1 teaspoon bottled hot sauce (choose a natural one with no sugar)
½ cup pureed silken tofu
Sea salt and cracked black pepper
2 cups cooked black beans, coarsely mashed with a fork (you may also use organic canned beans)
1 cup organic corn kernels (fresh or frozen)
Extra-virgin olive oil, for sautéing burgers

GREENS

2 teaspoons extra-virgin olive oil
4 to 5 kale leaves, washed, shredded
Sea salt

Whole-grain burger buns, for serving, toasted if desired
Sliced tomatoes, for serving

To make the burgers: Combine the red onion, bread crumbs, basil, jalapeño, mayonnaise, hot sauce, and pureed tofu in a mixing bowl. Season to taste with salt and pepper. Fold in the beans and corn until the ingredients are fully combined. Form the mixture into burger-sized patties. Arrange on a plate, cover, and refrigerate for 10 minutes so the patties firm up before cooking.

Heat a small amount of oil in a skillet over medium heat. Lay the patties in the skillet and cook until browned on both sides, about 4 minutes per side. Transfer to a plate, or if you like your burgers hot, place them on a baking sheet in a warm oven while you sauté the greens.

To make the greens: Heat the olive oil in the same skillet and sauté the kale until just wilted, about 2 minutes. Sprinkle with salt and sauté for 1 minute more.

To assemble, lay a burger on the bottom half of each bun, spoon some greens on top, and place a tomato slice on top of the greens. Spread the cut side of the top half of the buns with vegan mayo (if using) and press gently on top of the burgers. Serve immediately.

COOK'S TIP: *Use whatever condiments you desire to dress the burgers, from mustard to relish, sautéed mushrooms to sautéed onions.*

COOK'S TIP: *I learned this from my great friend Eric and I love this tip. To ensure that your burgers hold together (whatever recipe you're using), cut large onions in half crosswise and remove all the layers, leaving just the largest outer "rings." Press your burger mixture into the onion rings and proceed to fry, bake, or grill them. The burgers hold their shape and the onion softens and adds a bit more flavor.*

BREAKFAST SCRAMBLE

At breakfast, we break our fast after sleeping through the night. Served at the time of day when the body needs an easy wake-up and a chance to stabilize blood sugars, hard-to-digest foods like bacon and eggs or intense sweets like doughnuts jolt our delicate systems. Foods like these make us feel, at best, irritable, at worst, sluggish and lethargic. But here's a great dish for those of us who want heartier morning fare, giving us a centered energy for the day, with long-lasting endurance from the plant protein.

Makes 3 to 4 servings

1 teaspoon vegan butter substitute
1 teaspoon extra-virgin olive oil
1 small leek, split lengthwise, rinsed well, and thinly sliced (or 3 to 4 scallions, thinly sliced)
Sea salt
6 to 8 cremini mushrooms, brushed free of dirt, thinly sliced
1 carrot, julienned
½ roasted red bell pepper, thinly sliced (see Cook's Tip, page 113)
1 pound extra-firm tofu, coarsely crumbled
Generous pinch ground turmeric
2 tablespoons spring or filtered water
3 to 4 baby bok choy, rinsed well, bottoms removed, leaves separated from stems
2 to 3 sprigs fresh flatleaf parsley, coarsely chopped, for serving

Heat a dry skillet over medium heat. Melt the vegan butter with the olive oil and add the leek with a pinch of salt. Sauté the leek until limp, about 2 minutes. Add the mushrooms and a pinch of salt and sauté until the mushrooms release their juices and begin to reabsorb them. Add the carrot and roasted pepper with a pinch of salt and sauté for 1 minute.

Stir in the tofu and turmeric, season lightly with salt, and add the water. Cover and reduce the heat to low. Simmer, stirring frequently, for 3 to 5 minutes. Stir in the baby bok choy until the leaves just wilt. Serve hot, folding in the parsley just before serving.

COOK'S TIP: *Vary the vegetables as you desire, but keep them on the delicate side. I love adding finely shredded Brussels sprouts when they're in season. I also like to add fresh herbs, in season, for extra flavor.*

FRIED TOFU WITH BLACK BEAN SAUCE ON SCALLION PANCAKES

Once again, calm, cool tofu comes together with dramatic, spicy beans to create a centered focus, with vitality to burn. Dishes like this make you "simmer," so your energy doesn't fail you. Served over a simple scallion pancake, this dish needs only a fresh salad on the side.

Makes 4 to 5 servings

SCALLION PANCAKES

1 cup whole wheat pastry or sprouted whole wheat flour
½ teaspoon baking powder
¼ teaspoon sea salt
¼ cup plus 3 tablespoons avocado oil, divided
½ to ⅔ cup spring or filtered water
3 to 4 scallions, finely minced

FRIED TOFU

1 pound extra-firm tofu, cut into 1-inch cubes
Avocado or sunflower oil, for frying

BLACK BEAN SAUCE

2 teaspoons extra-virgin olive oil or avocado oil
1 jalapeño pepper, diced (do not seed)
1 red onion, diced
Sea salt
1 cup finely diced winter squash
1 cup organic corn kernels (fresh or frozen)
Dash organic soy sauce
2 cups cooked black turtle beans

2 to 3 fresh scallions, thinly sliced, for serving

To make the pancake batter: Combine the flour, baking powder, and salt in a bowl. Use a pastry blender or two knives to cut in ¼ cup of the oil until the mixture resembles coarse sand. Slowly mix in the water to create a thin (but not runny) pancake batter. Fold in the scallions. Cover and let the batter rest for 15 minutes before proceeding.

Meanwhile, make the tofu: Pat the tofu cubes dry. Heat about ¼ inch oil in a deep skillet and shallow fry the tofu until golden brown on all sides. Drain on paper towels and set aside.

To make the black bean sauce: Heat the oil in a skillet over medium-high heat. Sauté the jalapeño and onion with a pinch of salt for 1 minute. Add the winter squash and corn with a splash of soy sauce and sauté for 1 to 2 minutes more. Mash half the beans with a fork or potato masher and then stir them into the skillet with the remaining beans. Season lightly with soy sauce and add a small amount of spring or filtered water to loosen the mixture. Stir in the fried tofu cubes. Cover and simmer over very low heat for 5 to 7 minutes while you make the scallion pancakes.

To cook the pancakes, preheat the oven to 200°F. Heat a skillet over medium heat. Add the remaining 3 tablespoons oil. Drop tablespoons of batter into the hot oil to make 3-inch pancakes. Cook until golden brown, turning once to brown both sides. Transfer the pancakes to a baking sheet and then to the warm oven while making the remaining pancakes. You should be able to make 8 to 10 pancakes. »

» To serve, place 2 pancakes each on 4 to 5 individual plates. Top generously with tofu and black beans. Sprinkle with scallions and serve hot.

COOK'S TIP: *Use seasonal vegetables to vary this dish. In summer, swap out the winter squash for zucchini or yellow squash.*

QUINOA-ENCRUSTED TOFU ON SOBA

In this splendid main course, mild-mannered tofu is cooked sweet and spicy, "breaded" in cooked quinoa, and served over delicate soba noodles for a truly delicious main course.

Makes 2 to 3 servings

ENCRUSTED TOFU

1 cup natural ketchup
   (no sugar or artificial
   additives)
2 teaspoons hot sauce
Sea salt
1 pound extra-firm tofu,
   sliced in half lengthwise
   and then into 5 slices
   (10 slices total)
½ cup cooked quinoa

SOBA

8 ounces soba noodles
1 carrot, julienned
1 small bunch watercress,
   sliced into 1-inch pieces
1 red onion, cut in thin
   half-moons
2 teaspoons sesame oil
Dash organic soy sauce

Fresh lime juice, to taste

Preheat the oven to 425°F and line a baking sheet with parchment paper or a silicone mat. Place a wire rack on top.

To make the tofu: Mix together the ketchup, hot sauce, and salt to your taste. Dredge the tofu slices in the sauce and then in the cooked quinoa, pressing the quinoa onto the tofu (this is delightfully messy). Place the tofu pieces on the wire rack. Sprinkle any remaining quinoa on top of the tofu slices. Bake for 15 to 20 minutes, until the quinoa is crispy and lightly browned.

While the tofu cooks, make the soba: Bring a pot of salted water to a boil and cook the soba noodles according to package directions until al dente, about 10 minutes. Drain and rinse the noodles well to remove excess salt. Quickly toss the carrot, watercress, and onion with the warm noodles.

Heat the sesame oil in a deep skillet over medium heat. Add the noodle and vegetable mixture with a drizzle of soy sauce and cook, stirring, for 1 to 2 minutes, just to coat the noodles with the oil and soy sauce.

To serve, arrange the noodles and vegetables in large individual serving bowls. Drizzle with lime juice and top with the quinoa-crusted tofu slices. Serve hot.

SIMMERED TOFU AND VEGETABLES

Serve with a side of whole grain or a salad (or both) and you have a seriously satisfying meal. Miso is not just an exotic ingredient; it's also rich in the live enzymes and friendly bacteria that are essential to digestive health—the original probiotic, if you will. In this dish, it works deep in the body to strengthen digestion, leaving you feeling your oats.

Makes 3 to 4 servings

3 cups spring or filtered water
1 (3-inch) piece kombu
2 shallots or ½ red onion, diced
1 carrot, diced
1 cup diced daikon
1 cup small cauliflower florets
1 pound extra-firm tofu, cut into ½-inch cubes
1 tablespoon barley miso
2 stalks broccoli, cut into small florets
1 to 2 fresh scallions, thinly sliced on the diagonal, for serving

Combine the water, kombu, shallots, carrot, daikon, and cauliflower in a medium soup pot over medium heat. Cover and bring to a boil. Reduce the heat to low, add the tofu, and then cook until daikon is tender, about 15 minutes.

Remove a small amount of the broth and stir it into the miso to dissolve. Stir the miso back into the broth along with the broccoli. Simmer for 5 to 6 minutes, until the broccoli is crisp-tender. Take care not to boil the miso as this will destroy the enzymes.

To serve, spoon the vegetables, tofu, and broth into individual bowls and sprinkle with scallions. Serve hot.

TOFU AND WINTER SQUASH STEW

Tofu and sweet winter squash both have a character that can be relaxing to the body. Stewing makes us feel calm and centered; this long-simmered dish that promotes relaxation creates the perfect comfort food.

Makes 2 to 3 servings

1 onion, roughly diced
1 parsnip or carrot, cut into 1-inch chunks
1 small-medium butternut squash, seeded, cut into 1-inch pieces (do not peel)
8 ounces extra-firm tofu, cut into large cubes
Organic soy sauce, to taste
1 teaspoon brown rice syrup
1 cinnamon stick
1 to 2 teaspoons kuzu root or arrowroot powder, dissolved in a small amount of cold water

Layer the onion, parsnip or carrot, and winter squash in a deep pot. Add the tofu. Pour in enough spring or filtered water to reach a depth of ¼ inch. Sprinkle lightly with soy sauce, cover, and bring to a gentle boil over medium heat. Add the brown rice syrup and cinnamon stick. Cover, reduce the heat to low, and simmer until the squash is soft, about 25 minutes.

Season lightly with a little more soy sauce and remove the cinnamon stick. Cover and simmer for 5 minutes more. Stir in the dissolved kuzu root, gently stirring until a thin glaze forms over the stew. Transfer to a serving bowl and serve hot.

COOK'S TIP: *I often like to stir fresh chopped flatleaf parsley or scallions into this dish before serving to create a light, bright, balanced flavor.*

STIR-FRIED TEMPEH WITH BITTER GREENS

Tempeh pairs so well with bitter greens, as they both aid the body in digesting protein. As digestion is eased, you can use the protein more efficiently, creating stamina and vitality. A yummy and beneficial combination indeed!

Makes 3 to 4 servings

1 tablespoon avocado oil
½ red onion, cut into thin half-moons
Organic soy sauce, to taste
1 (1-inch) piece fresh ginger, juice extracted, pulp discarded (see Cook's Tip, page 54)
¼ teaspoon crushed red pepper flakes
1 small carrot, julienned
½ cup finely julienned daikon
8 ounces tempeh, cut into 1-inch slices
½ bunch broccoli rabe, rinsed well, chopped into 2-inch pieces

Heat a small amount of oil in a deep skillet or wok. Add the onion with a splash of soy sauce and stir-fry for 1 to 2 minutes, or until translucent. Add the ginger juice and red pepper flakes and stir well. Add the carrot and daikon with another splash of soy sauce and stir-fry for 1 to 2 minutes. Stir in the tempeh and a little more soy sauce and stir-fry for 4 to 5 minutes, lightly browning as evenly as possible. Finally, stir in the broccoli rabe, season lightly with soy sauce, and add a small amount of spring or filtered water (about 2 to 3 teaspoons) to steam the greens. Cover and steam over medium heat until the broccoli rabe is bright green, 2 to 3 minutes. Stir gently to combine and transfer to a serving platter. Serve immediately.

COOK'S TIP: *I like a squeeze of lemon juice as I serve this dish, but that's your choice. If you do, don't add the lemon until right before serving, as it will turn the greens an unappealing black if you add the juice and then wait to serve.*

TEMPEH REUBEN

The key to a good Reuben is in the Thousand Island dressing—in my view, anyway. A traditional Reuben is loaded with meat and cheese, but it's really the oozy, rich dressing we love so much. In this vegan version, you'll whip up a creamy dressing in no time from simple pantry ingredients. You'll never . . . and I mean never . . . buy bottled dressing again.

Makes 2 sandwiches

DRESSING

1 cup vegan mayonnaise substitute
⅓ cup natural ketchup (no sugar or artificial additives)
3 tablespoons natural sweet pickle relish
½ teaspoon garlic powder
½ teaspoon onion powder
Generous pinch sea salt

REUBEN

Avocado oil, for frying
8-ounce block tempeh, sliced in half and then in half widthwise, making 4 slender pieces
4 slices whole-grain rye bread
2 slices vegan Swiss cheese substitute (optional)
2 to 3 tablespoons natural sauerkraut

To make the dressing: Combine the mayonnaise, ketchup, pickle relish, garlic powder, onion powder, and salt in a bowl, adjusting the seasonings to your taste. Set aside.

To make the Reuben: Heat enough avocado oil in a skillet to cover the bottom of the pan and place over medium heat. Lay the tempeh slices in the hot oil and cook until browned, about 4 minutes. Turn and brown on the other side, about 4 minutes. Transfer to a plate. In the same skillet, lay the bread slices with the cheese on 2 of them (if using). Allow the cheese to melt as the bread toasts.

Remove the bread from the skillet and spread with dressing. Place 2 pieces of tempeh on top of the bread without cheese. Spoon the sauerkraut on top of the tempeh. Lay the bread with melted cheese on top to close the sandwiches. Slice diagonally and serve hot.

SEITAN KINPIRA

Strengthening and packed with protein, this dish is like rocket fuel in a bowl. The combination of burdock, the most strengthening root vegetable known to man, and carrot, another titan of power, with protein-packed seitan creates a dish that gives you a clear mind, sharp focus, and tremendous staying power.

Makes 2 to 3 servings

1 tablespoon avocado or extra-virgin olive oil
1 small yellow onion, cut into thin half-moons
Sea salt
1 cup julienned burdock
1 cup julienned carrot
8 ounces seitan, cut into 1-inch pieces
Dash organic soy sauce
1 teaspoon kuzu root, dissolved in a small amount of cold water
3 to 4 sprigs fresh flatleaf parsley, coarsely chopped
Dash brown rice vinegar

Heat the oil in skillet over medium-high heat. Sauté the onion with a pinch of salt until translucent, about 2 minutes. Add the burdock and a pinch of salt and sauté until shiny with oil. Spread the vegetables evenly over the skillet. Top with the carrot and then the seitan. Add spring or filtered water to just cover the burdock pieces. Cover and simmer for 5 minutes over medium-low heat. Season with soy sauce and simmer for 5 minutes more.

Remove the cover and stir in the dissolved kuzu, stirring until a clear glaze forms over the dish. Remove from the heat and stir in the parsley and a generous splash of rice vinegar. Transfer to a serving platter and serve immediately.

COOK'S TIP: *Usually, I give you the option of kuzu or arrowroot powder. However, in this recipe, I prefer you use kuzu if you can because the dish is designed to strengthen and alkalize digestion and kuzu is more effective at supporting this than arrowroot. But if arrowroot is all you have, then go with it.*

CHAPTER 7

KILLER DESSERTS THAT WON'T KILL YOU

I read an interview with Maida Heatter, the idol of every dessert maker, back when I was learning to cook. Her words have stayed with me to this day. The interviewer asked her if she loved cooking as much as she loved baking and making desserts. She replied, with her characteristic wit, that she liked cooking just fine—it was like the warm-up to a baseball game.

I have always loved to make desserts, even working at it professionally at one point in my career. As much as I enjoy all aspects of cooking, delicious and beautiful desserts really bring out my creative side. Cooking is often just the opening act for me.

You can imagine my dismay when I changed my style of eating to whole, unprocessed foods. No sugar, no milk, no butter, no refined flours, which meant no crème caramel, no buttercream frostings, no custards. And, I thought, no desserts unless I was supposed to consider those hockey-puck cookies and paperweight muffins I had found in natural foods stores to be a treat. It was a grim thought.

So I struggled with healthy dessert recipes that tasted like, well, healthy desserts; they were not worth the work and certainly not worth the calories. And then one day, as I threw yet another batch of cookies in the trash, I had an epiphany—one of many in my life, which often come to me when I'm in the kitchen. Why was I struggling so much? I was a pastry chef. The ingredients may have changed, but the techniques remained the same. I didn't need to reinvent the wheel. This wasn't rocket science. We're talking cookies here. I took a deep breath, pulled out some of my most cherished recipes from my own career and my mother's kitchen, and went to work.

I made a lot of discoveries as I experimented. I found that I didn't like the flavor that apple juice gave as a sweetener, except in apple cake or apple pie. I fell in love with whole wheat pastry flour and sprouted whole wheat flour, made from a softer wheat, yielding a lighter pastry, yet retaining its whole-grain flour status. I continue to adore sprouted whole wheat flour, which digests in the body more like a vegetable than a grain, and gives me the lightest cakes and cookies I could ever imagine making.

I began my passionate affair with complex carbohydrate sweeteners like brown rice syrup and coconut sugar that don't drastically alter the glucose balance in the blood. I discovered the wonder of grain, nut, and soy milks. All my playing in the kitchen paid off. I rediscovered delicious, sweet, decadent-tasting desserts that didn't compromise my commitment to healthy eating. I could make killer desserts, but they wouldn't kill me. Life was good again.

I made an even more important discovery. I discovered that we need dessert . . . yes, *need* dessert. In whole foods cooking, we say that nothing is arbitrary, that everything is done for a reason; everything will have an effect on us—how we look, feel, and act. It's no different with dessert. It, too, has a purpose in our lives. Just like broccoli.

Dessert (good-quality dessert, at least) works to relax the body and make us feel happy, at least when we're not torturing ourselves and feeling guilty about eating it. Dessert can relieve tension in the body, relax tight muscles, and, in small amounts, eaten regularly, can actually help us eat less and not crave sweets. Think about it. On a deadline at work? Exhausted? Stressed? Depressed? In most cases, you reach for sweets, naturally, in an attempt to release the tension and lift your spirits.

But wait. Can dessert really help you eat less? It works like this. Just because you deprive yourself of dessert, it doesn't mean that your body doesn't want or need sweet tastes and richness. In the body's search for satisfaction, you will eat more food. You know the drill. There's one cookie left but you just shouldn't. So you have a piece of fresh fruit. But the cookie calls you. So you have a handful of nuts. The cookie's still there. You top it off with a rice cake with peanut butter . . . and the cookie!

Treat yourself to a good-quality dessert a few times a week, and you'll find that you spend fewer nights with your head in the refrigerator looking for just the right something to satisfy you.

How much dessert is healthy? Take a page from the maddeningly fit European women who seem to enjoy desserts at will and remain slender and healthy. They know the secret and I'll share it with you. It's so simple, you'll wonder why you wasted all those months and years avoiding sweets. Ready? After three bites, you simply don't taste sweet flavor anymore. So they stop at three bites, savoring each morsel for intense satisfaction. They are having their cake and eating it too. And so can you. I call it the Three Bite Rule and it has served me so well over the years.

Go ahead, indulge yourself with three bites: a cookie or two, a sliver of pie, maybe even a miniature custard-filled tart. Made from whole, natural ingredients, dessert can serve your needs for richness, satisfaction, and unparalleled joy, at least where food is concerned.

But what about the complications of making dessert? Isn't baking an alchemy reserved for the finest chef or a domestic goddess type like Nigella Lawson or Martha Stewart? I used to think so. I grew up in a family of passionate Italian bakers. My mother, grandmother, and aunts were always "competing" for the title of the family's best baker. As I stood by each of them, trying to glean their techniques and wisdom for my own sweet creations, I was always a little stymied . . . and frustrated.

They did as they pleased with a recipe. They didn't sift, whisk, or fold. Measure? Nope. As I peppered them with questions, I had no idea that they were teaching me with each enigmatic answer. "The batter will tell you when it's ready," they would say. "You'll know when the dough is right." I was so frustrated.

When I became a professional, my first executive pastry chef was French. Finally, I would have the instruction I craved. The French knew how to bake, not like my freewheeling Italian relatives. As it turned out, he didn't sift, whisk, or fold. And measure? Nope. I have since discovered that this chef was a rarity and that most great pastry chefs do, in fact, whisk, measure, fold, and follow all the guidelines for successful baking, but it seemed I had good karma and found a teacher who was my kind of baker. I had to discover and study techniques on my own, which I did. And now, some rules I follow and some I don't. I learned to bake with passion, not chemistry.

As I converted recipes over the years, I often smile as I think of the treats prepared by my family. With flour measured with "the blue lid" and oil with "the little red scoop," I recreated family treasures with a healthy twist.

I discovered that my crazy relatives were right. Baking is driven by a passion for the art of it, not so much by the chemistry of the ingredients. Of course, the chemistry plays an important part, but I think it's a marriage of the two that creates the perfect dessert.

Now before you run off, driven by passion to create desserts, let's talk about some basic techniques that you need to become familiar with to successfully create delicious desserts. As I stood at my relatives' elbows, I didn't realize I was getting tutorials on how batter should look, feel, smell, and taste. I didn't realize all their little quirks of baking were actually valid tips on how to achieve the best results.

If you're not a baker, then I will suggest you follow a recipe closely for the first go-round of a treat. Consider it your "apprenticeship" with an Italian relative. But remember, when I say to follow a recipe, I don't mean with your shoulders hiked up around your ears with a trembling measuring spoon over a bowl. That won't drive your passion. Read the recipe; get familiar with it and give it a go. Start with something simple, like cookies or muffins. Save showpiece cakes and pie crusts until you have built your confidence and feel like stretching your baking limits.

Just don't get trapped in the rules of the recipe. I received a cookbook in the mail that supposedly would help me create the perfect cookie. The recipes were great and easily converted to healthy and vegan, which is an indication of a great recipe . . . that it can be adapted. Here's where the book lost me. Each cookie recipe had a section on why the recipe worked, with strict (and I mean hard-line) rules not to be changed or altered should you want your cookies to succeed. I remember reading it and thinking that these were cookies for God's sake, not world peace. Cookies—friendly, casual, comforting, rustic cookies—and this book had my shoulders up around my ears with stress, and I was just *reading* the recipes. That said, I use the book all the time as inspiration. A glance at a page, a cookie name, or a recipe, and I am off to spin my own version of classic and unique cookies, with my years of experience serving me very well.

MY SECRETS TO SUCCESS

I'll tell you my secrets when it comes to baking. There are only a few, but I hope they serve you as they have served me.

I am deeply and passionately in love with my stand mixer and use it for just about every baked dessert. I always whip together my fat and sweetener, even when the recipe tells me otherwise. I then slowly add the flour, leavening, salt, and spices (if I am using them), plus any other flavorings, and mix again. Then I add whatever liquid is required (if any) to create the dough or batter consistency I want. Finally, I gently pulse in the nuts, seeds, chocolate chips, fruit, or whatever else I am adding. One machine, one bowl. Then I scoop, spoon, or pour the batter or dough into the appropriate vessel and bake until done, based on what the recipe might advise. You can also use a hand mixer to achieve the batter or dough you want.

When it comes to the actual baking, take care. Everyone's oven is calibrated a bit differently, so you must learn your oven in order to recognize when your treat is done. Are the cookies slightly tender in the center? Take them out if you want chewy cookies;

leave them for one to two minutes more if you like cookies that are crispier. Does the center of your cake or your muffins spring back to the touch? Get them out of the oven! Is your pie crust lightly browned at the edges and firm to the touch? It's done.

Ingredients are where people struggle with baking . . . what, where, how, and why? I always say that anyone can bake vegan desserts with white flour and sugar. The real challenge is creating desserts that are killer good but healthy for us.

I struggled for years to find the perfect ingredients for my baking and I never, ever, ever deviate from these certain items. It's not that I am usually so brand loyal, but I'm using what has been proven to work so that I don't worry or fret about a recipe result. My trusted ingredients serve me so well, every . . . single . . . time, so I can go off and bake with passion, not stress over the "what if's" of any particular treat.

When it comes to sweeteners, I rely on two for nearly every recipe. They work fabulously well and give me great flavor and texture without compromising wellness. I use coconut sugar and brown rice syrup, both manufactured by Suzanne's Specialties (suzannes-specialties.com). You can get organic coconut sugar just about anywhere, but I love the fine granulation of Suzanne's Specialties. I never have to regrind it when I need a finer sugar. And the brown rice syrup? It's the only brand I use. Yes, there are other fine brands, all organic with no arsenic in the final product, but Suzanne's Specialties produces their syrup the traditional way, with a cultured rice called koji. Why is this important? Most other syrups are produced with enzymes, and though they are natural, I have discovered that these enzymes can neutralize the leavening in baked goods, resulting in sunken cakes and mushy cupcakes. I never have that experience with Suzanne's Specialties, so I am brand loyal to a fault. I can count on my results and that counts with me.

Chocolate was like the Holy Grail for me. I want to enjoy the health benefits of the best-quality dark chocolate, but at the same time, I want to do the best for the people who produce chocolate. I want as little sugar as possible; I want it to be Fair Trade, ensuring farmers and producers earn a fair wage, use no child labor, and that the environment is protected. And most of all, I want great flavor.

My closest friend in the world, Cynthia, called me one day a few years ago and announced that she was producing a unique take on chocolate and couldn't wait for me to taste it. Okay, I thought. She announced that she was the brains behind the chocolate brand, Lily's Sweets Chocolate (lilyssweets.com), a line of eating and baking chocolate that is Fair Trade, with no added sugar because it is sweetened with stevia. *Oh no,* I thought (seriously, that was in my head). Stevia is a wonderful, healthy, no-calorie sweetener, but usually comes with the baggage of a metallic aftertaste that is a bit off-putting.

But she's my closest friend, so I vowed to suck it up and lie, saying I loved it, regardless of the stevia-ness of the chocolate. I bit into a bar and was treated to creamy

GINGER-POACHED PEARS

The delicate sweet taste of pears is showcased in this simple and beautiful dessert. To gentle the effect of the fruit sugar on our blood chemistry, the pears are poached in a lightly spiced broth, with ginger for strength, cinnamon for warmth, and lemon to aid the body in assimilating the sugars. The overall effect is a dessert that relaxes and nourishes the body.

Makes 4 servings

1 (1-inch) piece fresh ginger, thinly sliced
4 ripe pears with stems, unpeeled
1 cinnamon stick
3 tablespoons mirin or white wine
Grated zest of 1 lemon
¼ cup Suzanne's Specialties brown rice syrup

Place the ginger in the bottom of a pot that will hold the pears snugly. Take a thin slice off the bottom of each pear so it will sit flat. Arrange the pears on top of the ginger. Add enough spring or filtered water to cover the pears; add the cinnamon stick, mirin, lemon zest, and rice syrup. Cover and bring to a boil. Turn off the heat, remove the cover, and drape cheesecloth, a very thin kitchen towel, or a clean bandanna over the surface of the water to keep the pears submerged. Let cool to room temperature. Remove the pears and arrange, on flat ends, on a plate.

Strain the pear cooking liquid, reserving 2 cups and discarding the rest. Bring the reserved liquid to a boil over medium heat, and boil until reduced by half and slightly thickened.

Spoon the thickened sauce over the pears, and serve immediately. These will keep, in a tightly sealed container in the refrigerator, for about 2 days.

COOK'S TIP: *For added richness, I often melt ½ cup Lily's Dark Chocolate Premium Baking Chips and place a little pool of chocolate sauce under each pear and then spoon the reduced sauce over the top of each pear.*

SPICED PECAN BAKED APPLES

Baking fruit introduces a strengthening energy that is the perfect complement to the strong sweetness that is the nature of fruit. Eating a lot of raw fruit can leave us feeling tired, weak, and chilled. Fruit is mostly sugar and water. Cooking, especially baking, introduces the vitality of fire for strength and warmth, gentles the sugars, and creates a satisfying sweet dessert. In this dish, the nuts add lots of energy, providing a balancing counterpoint to the relaxed fruit. Now you know why fruit and nuts go so well together.

Makes 6 servings

6 large apples (Red Delicious, Golden Delicious, or Rome)
1 cup pecan pieces
⅓ cup raisins
¼ cup unsweetened shredded coconut
2 tablespoons Suzanne's Specialties brown rice syrup
Grated zest and juice of 1 lemon
Grated zest of 1 orange
¼ teaspoon powdered ginger
About 6 tablespoons fruit-sweetened apricot preserves
6 whole pecans
1 cup unfiltered apple juice
2 teaspoons avocado or extra-virgin olive oil

Preheat the oven to 375°F.

Core the apples, but do not peel. Cut a thin slice off the bottom of each apple so it will sit flat. With a sharp paring knife, make a 1-inch-wide by 1-inch-deep hollow in the top of each apple. Arrange the apples in a deep baking dish.

Coarsely mince the pecan pieces, raisins, and coconut. Mix them together in a medium bowl, then stir in the rice syrup, lemon and orange zests, and ginger. Fill the hollow of each apple abundantly with the pecan mixture. Spoon a dollop of preserves over the top of each apple, and press a whole pecan on top of the preserves.

Combine the apple juice and oil in a saucepan and cook over medium heat for 2 to 3 minutes. Remove from the heat and stir in the lemon juice. Spoon into the baking dish around the apples and cover loosely with foil.

Bake, basting every 10 minutes with the juice, for about 35 minutes, or until the apples are tender. Serve warm, with any remaining juices spooned over the top. These will keep, in a tightly sealed container in the refrigerator, for 2 to 3 days.

LEMON STARS

Adapted from a sweet cream cheese dough, these delectable cookies are richly satisfying yet incredibly light, so they won't weigh you down, as tender cookies are easier to digest. Add to that the sparkle of lemon zest and the energy of poppy seeds, and you have created a cookie that makes the perfect dessert.

Makes about 48 cookies

2 cups whole wheat pastry or sprouted whole wheat flour

2 to 3 tablespoons poppy seeds

2 tablespoons coconut sugar

1 teaspoon baking powder

½ teaspoon baking soda

Pinch sea salt

¼ cup avocado or extra-virgin olive oil

4 ounces silken tofu

Grated zest of 1 lemon

1 teaspoon pure vanilla extract

¾ cup Suzanne's Specialties brown rice syrup, divided

Combine the flour, poppy seeds, coconut sugar, baking powder, baking soda, and salt in a large bowl. Puree the oil and tofu in a food processor fitted with the metal blade or in a blender until smooth. Fold the tofu mixture into the flour along with the lemon zest, vanilla, and ½ cup of the rice syrup. Stir until combined into a soft dough. If the dough seems dry, add lemon juice or water for moisture. Divide the dough in half and pat each piece into a thick disk.

Preheat the oven to 350°F. Line four baking sheets with parchment paper.

Divide the dough into quarters. Wrap the three pieces you're not using right away to prevent drying. Roll the remaining piece out on a lightly floured surface to an ⅛-inch thickness. With a star-shaped cookie cutter, cut out cookies and transfer to the prepared pans, leaving about 1 inch between cookies. Repeat with the remaining dough.

As soon as two of the baking sheets are filled with cookies, bake them for 10 to 12 minutes, or until golden at the edges and firm; do not overbake or the cookies will become quite hard as they cool. Repeat with the remaining dough.

To glaze the lemon stars, heat the remaining ¼ cup rice syrup in a small pan over high heat until it foams. Quickly spoon over the warm cookies. These will keep, in a tightly sealed container, for 6 to 7 days.

BACI DI DAMAS (LADIES' KISSES)

These crisp on the outside, tender on the inside sandwich cookies are each just one bite of richness with deep rich chocolate at the center. And just like ladies' kisses, they'll leave you wanting more.

Makes about 40 sandwiches (80 cookies)

COOKIES

5 tablespoons vegan butter substitute, cold
½ cup coconut sugar
1 teaspoon pure vanilla extract
Pinch sea salt
1 cup finely ground almond or hazelnut meal
2 tablespoons arrowroot powder
½ teaspoon baking soda
½ cup whole wheat pastry or sprouted whole wheat flour

CHOCOLATE FILLING

1 ounce Lily's Dark Chocolate Premium Baking Chips
2 teaspoons Suzanne's Specialties brown rice syrup

Preheat the oven to 350°F and position the oven racks in the middle and lower middle of the oven. Line two rimmed baking sheets with parchment.

To make the cookies: In a stand mixer (or using a handheld mixer), cream the cold vegan butter with the coconut sugar, vanilla, and sea salt until smooth. Add the almond or hazelnut meal, arrowroot, baking soda, and flour. Mix until a soft dough forms, taking care not to overmix. Turn the dough out onto a dry work surface and create a soft ball. Cut the dough into 4 equal pieces.

Roll each piece into a rope about 10 inches long and about ½ inch thick. Cut the rope into ¼-inch pieces. Roll each piece into a ball and arrange on a prepared baking sheet about 1 inch apart. Repeat with the remaining dough. You should have about 80 small balls of dough on the baking sheets.

Bake for 10 to 12 minutes, rotating the pans halfway through baking, at 5-6 minutes. The cookies should be a wee bit soft to the touch. Transfer the cookies to cooling racks and cool completely.

When the cookies are cooled, make the chocolate filling: Melt the chocolate and rice syrup in a heat-resistant bowl over simmering water (make sure the bowl doesn't touch the water), whisking often, until the chocolate is creamy, smooth, and shiny. Transfer the bowl to a dry towel on your work surface. Pairing cookies of similar size, spoon ¼ teaspoon of filling on the flat side of a cookie and gently press the flat side of the other cookie into the chocolate, creating a tiny sandwich, or "kiss." Repeat with all the cookies and chocolate. These will keep, in a tightly sealed container, for about 12 days.

COOK'S TIP: *If the chocolate thickens while you are working, simply loosen it over simmering water for a few seconds and continue.*

PEANUT BUTTER MARVELS

These chewy treats are quite decadent tasting. No one will guess they're actually healthy.

Makes about 24 cookies

½ cup unsalted, unsweetened, chunky peanut butter

8 tablespoons vegan butter substitute, softened

5 tablespoons coconut sugar

¼ cup Suzanne's Specialties brown rice syrup

2 teaspoons pure vanilla extract

Pinch sea salt

1½ cups whole wheat pastry or sprouted whole wheat flour

½ cup rolled oats

¼ cup unsweetened flaked coconut

½ teaspoon baking powder

½ teaspoon baking soda

⅔ cup Lily's Dark Chocolate Premium Baking Chips

Preheat the oven to 350°F. Line two baking sheets with parchment paper.

Whip the peanut butter, vegan butter, coconut sugar, brown rice syrup, vanilla, and salt in a medium bowl until smooth and creamy. Add the flour, rolled oats, coconut, baking powder, and baking soda to the peanut butter mixture and mix into a soft dough. Fold in the chocolate chips to incorporate them fully.

Drop rounded tablespoonfuls of dough onto the prepared pans, pressing lightly and rounding, leaving 1 inch between cookies. Bake for 14 to 15 minutes, or until the cookies are light golden and tenderly firm. Transfer to wire racks and cool completely. These will keep, in a tightly sealed container, for about 10 days.

HAMANTASCHEN

A cookie traditionally used in the celebration of Purim, hamantaschen have come to symbolize the emotions of this Jewish holiday—pure merriment and joy. Just one look at this festive, richly filled pastry and you'll know what I mean. Although tradition calls for a poppy seed or prune filling, modern hamantaschen are often filled with apricots or cherries (my personal favorite). No matter what the filling, these soft, delicious pastries will leave you happy and relaxed.

Makes about 24 cookies

PASTRY

2 cups whole wheat pastry or sprouted whole wheat flour

¼ cup coconut sugar

2 teaspoons baking powder

2 teaspoons grated lemon zest

⅛ teaspoon sea salt

½ cup vegan butter substitute

1 teaspoon pure vanilla extract

½ to ⅔ cup spring or filtered water

DRIED CHERRY FILLING

1½ cups unsweetened dried cherries, soaked in warm water until tender and drained well

Grated zest of 1 orange

⅓ cup fresh orange juice

1 teaspoon Suzanne's Specialties brown rice syrup

Pinch sea salt

To make the pastry: Process the flour, coconut sugar, baking powder, lemon zest, and salt in a food processor fitted with the metal blade until combined. Add the vegan butter and vanilla and pulse 45 to 50 times, or until the mixture is the texture of wet sand. Do not overmix. Slowly pour in a thin stream of water, a little at a time, pulsing just until the dough gathers into a ball. Wrap the dough in plastic wrap and chill 1 for hour.

To make the filling: Combine the dried cherries, orange zest and juice, brown rice syrup, and salt in a saucepan. Simmer over low heat until a thick, stewlike consistency forms, 7 to 10 minutes. Transfer to a bowl and cool completely before making the cookies.

Preheat the oven to 350°F. Line two baking sheets with parchment paper.

Roll out half of the dough on a floured surface or between parchment sheets to a ¼-inch thickness. With a 3-inch cookie cutter or glass, cut out rounds of dough. Transfer the rounds to the prepared pans, leaving about ½ inch between cookies. Spoon a teaspoon of filling into the center of each round. Fold up and pinch the edges to form triangular-shaped cookies, with the filling peeking out of the center. Pinch the dough firmly, so the seams don't come open. Repeat with the remaining dough and filling.

Bake the cookies for about 20 minutes, or until lightly golden and firm. Cool on the baking sheet for 5 minutes, »

» and then transfer to wire racks to cool completely. These will keep, in a tightly sealed container, for about 4 days.

COOK'S TIP: *Melt ½ cup Lily's Dark Chocolate Premium Baking Chips and spread on the dough before the cherry filling to create a cherry-chocolate flavor that is out of this world.*

COCOA MADELEINES

I have loved buttery madeleines for as long as I can remember. Their tender, almost creamy texture can make me swoon. But I have not been able to replicate that tender, cakelike cookie . . . until now! Enjoy!

Makes 12 madeleines

2 tablespoons arrowroot powder
6 tablespoons spring or filtered water
⅓ cup vegan butter substitute, melted and cooled
1 teaspoon pure vanilla extract
1 cup coconut sugar
¾ cup whole wheat pastry or sprouted whole wheat flour
1 tablespoon unsweetened cocoa powder
¼ teaspoon baking powder
Pinch sea salt

Preheat the oven to 350°F and oil a madeleine pan very well. (A madeleine pan is specific, with shell-like cups to hold the cookies. You can get one in most kitchen stores.)

In a mixing bowl, combine the arrowroot with the water until smooth with no lumps. Mix in the vegan butter and vanilla. Whisk in the coconut sugar, flour, cocoa powder, baking powder, and salt until a smooth batter forms. It will be quite loose.

Spoon about 2 tablespoons batter into each madeleine cup, but do not overfill. Bake for 14 minutes, or until the cookies spring back to the touch. Cool completely before turning out of the madeleine pan.

These will keep, in a sealed container, for about a week before they grow too soggy to be enjoyable.

COOK'S TIP: *Bring ½ cup unsweetened almond milk to a boil and pour over 1 cup Lily's Dark Chocolate Premium Baking Chips to create a lovely chocolate glaze to dip the cookies' edges in for added chocolaty richness.*

APPLE-CRANBERRY CRISP

Sweet and tart fruit covered by a tender, cakelike topping is one of the most wonderful, homey desserts. Easy to make, delicious, and beautiful—you get it all with this one. Baking the fruit gentles its simple sugars, and the topping gives you the satisfaction of flour without eating too much of it. The tart flavor of the cranberries balances the sweet apples perfectly.

Makes about 8 servings

FRUIT FILLING

3 to 4 Granny Smith apples, peeled, cored, and thinly sliced

¾ cup unsweetened dried cranberries

1 tablespoon avocado or extra-virgin olive oil, plus more for the pan

2 tablespoons arrowroot powder

2 tablespoons Suzanne's Specialties brown rice syrup

TOPPING

1 cup whole wheat pastry or sprouted whole wheat flour

½ cup rolled oats

1 teaspoon baking powder

1 teaspoon ground allspice

½ teaspoon ground ginger

⅛ teaspoon sea salt

½ cup Suzanne's Specialties brown rice syrup

¼ cup avocado or extra-virgin olive oil

About ½ cup unsweetened almond, soy, or other nondairy milk

½ cup coarsely minced pecans

Preheat the oven to 350°F. Lightly oil a 9-inch square baking dish.

To make the filling: Mix the apples and cranberries with the oil until coated. Stir in the arrowroot powder and brown rice syrup and spread evenly in the prepared pan.

To make the topping: Combine the flour, oats, baking powder, allspice, ginger, and sea salt in a medium bowl. Mix in the brown rice syrup and oil to make a soft dough. Slowly mix in the milk to make a thick, spoonable batter. Fold in the pecans.

Spoon the topping, by dollops, over the surface of the fruit, covering it almost completely, but allowing some fruit to peek through.

Bake for 30 to 35 minutes, or until the fruit is bubbling and the topping is golden and firm. Serve warm.

APPLE STREUSEL TART

Pies and tarts are among our culture's favorite desserts. We love everything about them: the flaky crust, rich fillings, sweet toppings, ease of preparation, and, best of all, their homey, comfortable energy. We love a piece of apple or pumpkin pie in cold weather, and nothing says summer to us quite like blueberry, cherry, or peach pie.

Makes 10 to 12 servings

PASTRY

1¾ cups whole wheat pastry or sprouted whole wheat flour
⅛ teaspoon sea salt
½ cup avocado or extra-virgin olive oil, plus more for the pan
About ¼ cup spring or filtered water

STREUSEL TOPPING

1½ cups whole wheat pastry or sprouted whole wheat flour
½ cup coarsely minced pecans
¼ cup coconut sugar
2 tablespoons avocado or extra-virgin olive oil

APPLE FILLING

6 Granny Smith apples, left unpeeled, cored and thinly sliced
Grated zest and juice of 1 lemon
3 tablespoons Suzanne's Specialties brown rice syrup
2 tablespoons arrowroot powder
2 tablespoons avocado or extra-virgin olive oil
Pinch sea salt

Preheat the oven to 350°F. Lightly oil a 13-inch tart pan with a removable bottom, taking care to oil all crevices.

To make the pastry: Combine the flour and salt in a medium bowl. Cut in the oil with a pastry blender or two knives until the mixture is the texture of wet sand. Slowly mix in the water until the dough just gathers together; do not overmix. Gather the dough into a ball, cover with a damp towel, and let it rest for 5 minutes to relax the gluten.

Roll the dough out between two sheets of parchment paper into a 14-inch round. Gently transfer to the prepared pan and, without stretching the dough, press it into the pan, fitting it into all the crevices. Pierce in several places with a fork.

Bake for 8 to 10 minutes, or until pale golden. Set aside, leaving the oven on.

To make the topping: Combine the flour, pecans, coconut sugar, and oil in a small bowl and stir to form a coarse, granular texture. Set aside.

To make the filling: Combine the apples, lemon zest and juice, brown rice syrup, arrowroot powder, oil, and salt in a large bowl.

Spread the filling evenly over the partially baked shell. Crumble the topping over the filling, covering it completely. Bake for 45 to 50 minutes, or until the apples are soft and the topping is golden and crunchy. Cool for about 15 minutes before slicing.

This will keep, in a tightly sealed container, for about 2 days before the crust gets soggy.

COOK'S TIP: *If your crust is browning too quickly, cover the pie with a loose foil tent. Uncover for the last 10 minutes of baking to brown the topping.*

» Cool the cake in the pan for 10 minutes, then invert onto a serving platter. Leave the pan over the cake for 1 minute before removing it to prevent the pears from sticking; if they do, simply replace them on top of the cake.

To serve, whisk the lemon sauce to loosen and slice the cake into wedges. Serve the warm cake on a pool of cool lemon sauce.

MOCHA CAKE WITH CHOCOLATE GANACHE

A rich coffee-flavored cake smothered in chocolate ganache is a decadent treat. I am a firm believer that we need decadence now and then; otherwise, life becomes a grim endurance. Spicy and moist, this cake will satisfy your need for richness without compromising your idea of healthy eating.

Makes 10 to 12 servings

CAKE

2½ cups whole wheat pastry or sprouted whole wheat flour

3 tablespoons coconut sugar

1 tablespoon baking powder

1 teaspoon baking soda

⅛ teaspoon sea salt

2 teaspoons finely ground espresso or 1 tablespoon coffee flour

¼ cup avocado or extra-virgin olive oil

½ cup Suzanne's Specialties brown rice syrup

1 teaspoon pure vanilla extract

½ cup Lily's Dark Chocolate Premium Baking Chips

1 cup unsweetened almond, soy, or other nondairy milk

GANACHE

⅔ cup Lily's Dark Chocolate Premium Baking Chips

¼ cup unsweetened almond, soy, or other nondairy milk

2 tablespoons Suzanne's Specialties brown rice syrup

1 teaspoon pure vanilla extract

Apricot Roses, for serving (optional, see Cook's Tip)

To make the cake: Preheat the oven to 350°F. Lightly oil and flour a 10-inch Bundt pan.

Combine the flour, coconut sugar, baking powder, baking soda, salt, and ground espresso in a large bowl. Mix in the oil, brown rice syrup, and vanilla. Warm the chocolate chips and milk in a small saucepan over low heat, stirring until melted and combined. Stir the chocolate into the flour mixture to make a thick, smooth cake batter. Spoon evenly into the prepared pan.

Bake for about 35 minutes, until the center springs back to the touch. Cool the cake in the pan for about 10 minutes. Invert onto a serving plate and cool completely before frosting.

To make the ganache: When you're ready to glaze the cake, place the chocolate chips in a heat-resistant bowl. Heat the milk, brown rice syrup, and vanilla in a small saucepan over medium heat until very foamy. Pour the milk mixture over the chocolate chips, whisking to make a creamy, smooth ganache. Spoon over the cake, allowing the chocolate to run down the sides of the cake. Decorate with apricot roses, if desired.

COOK'S TIP: APRICOT ROSES *For 4 apricot roses, you will need 16 dried apricots (unsulfured, from a natural foods store). Roll and flatten 4 apricots to form 2-inch circles. Lay a flattened apricot on a dry surface. Lay a second one on top, overlapping by about ¾ inch. Overlap the third and fourth apricots in the same way. Press the bottom edges together with a rolling pin. Roll up the row of apricots as tightly as possible. Press the base flat with your fingers, and trim flat with a* »

» *sharp knife. Insert a toothpick into the base, trimming to leave about ¼ inch exposed. Holding the "rose" by the base, gently fold the petals open to form a rose shape. Press the rose into the top of the cake, inserting the exposed toothpick into the cake to hold it in place. The roses will keep, in a sealed container at room temperature, for about a week.*

SWEET FRUIT PIZZA

This is a comfortable, rustic dessert that is just perfect for casually lazy get-togethers. The flaky biscuit crust is a wonderful complement to the sweet, succulent summer fruit mounded on the surface. Topped with an apricot glaze, this homey tart strikes the perfect laid-back note.

Makes 8 to 10 servings

PIZZA

2½ cups whole wheat pastry or sprouted whole wheat flour

1 tablespoon baking powder

⅛ teaspoon sea salt

5 tablespoons avocado or extra-virgin olive oil, divided

¼ cup plus ¼ cup Suzanne's Specialties brown rice syrup, divided

½ to ⅔ cup unsweetened almond, soy, or other nondairy milk

1 small plum, halved, pitted, and thinly sliced

1 to 2 peaches, left unpeeled, halved, pitted, and thinly sliced

½ cup fresh raspberries

½ cup thinly sliced strawberries

½ cup blueberries or blackberries

GLAZE

½ cup fruit-sweetened apricot preserves

2 tablespoons Suzanne's Specialties brown rice syrup

To make the pizza: Preheat the oven to 350°F. Line a 10-inch pizza pan with parchment paper or lightly coat with oil.

Combine the flour, baking powder, and salt in a food processor fitted with the metal blade. Add 4 tablespoons of the oil and ¼ cup of the rice syrup; pulse 45 to 50 times, or until the mixture is the texture of wet sand. Slowly add the milk through the feed tube and pulse until the dough gathers into a ball.

Roll the dough between two sheets of parchment paper or on a dry, lightly floured surface into a 9- to 10-inch round. Place in the prepared pan.

Place all the fruit in a medium mixing bowl. Gently stir in the remaining 1 tablespoon oil and remaining ¼ cup rice syrup to coat the fruit. Spread the fruit evenly over the surface of the dough, leaving ½ inch around the rim uncovered.

Bake for 25 to 30 minutes, or until the fruit is lightly browned and bubbling. Remove from the oven and transfer to a serving plate.

To make the glaze: Heat the preserves and brown rice syrup in a small pot over high heat until the mixture foams. Quickly spoon over the warm pizza, and allow to stand for about 15 minutes to set the glaze. Slice into wedges to serve.

PUMPKIN SQUARES

Pumpkin pie filling atop a flaky biscuit crust is so homey and appealing. I prefer these creamy little squares to a traditional pumpkin pie. Bite-size, rich, and spicy, these are perfect with a hot cup of tea as a cozy treat. Easier to make than a pie, this is the perfect stepping-stone to pie making.

Makes 12 to 16 bars

BISCUIT CRUST

1½ cups whole wheat pastry or sprouted whole wheat flour
¼ cup avocado or extra-virgin olive oil, plus more for the pan
2 tablespoons coconut sugar
1 teaspoon baking powder
Pinch sea salt
¼ to ½ cup unsweetened almond, soy, or other nondairy milk

PUMPKIN FILLING

2 cups unsweetened pureed sugar pumpkin or butternut squash
1 cup unsweetened almond, soy, or other nondairy milk
¼ cup Suzanne's Specialties brown rice syrup
2 tablespoons agar flakes
1 teaspoon pure vanilla extract
½ teaspoon ground ginger
¼ teaspoon ground cinnamon
¼ teaspoon freshly grated nutmeg
Pinch sea salt
2 tablespoons kuzu root or arrowroot powder, dissolved in ¼ cup cold water

PECAN TOPPING

¼ cup Suzanne's Specialties brown rice syrup
1 cup coarsely minced pecan pieces

To make the crust: Preheat the oven to 350°F. Lightly oil a 9- or 10-inch square baking dish.

Combine the flour, oil, coconut sugar, baking powder, and salt in a food processor fitted with the metal blade. Pulse 40 to 50 times, or until the mixture is the texture of wet sand. Slowly add the milk through the feed tube, and pulse until the mixture gathers into a ball. Press the dough evenly into the prepared dish.

Bake for 12 minutes. Set aside, leaving the oven on.

To make the filling: Combine the squash or pumpkin, milk, brown rice syrup, agar flakes, vanilla, ginger, cinnamon, nutmeg, and salt in a saucepan. Cook over low heat, stirring frequently, until the agar dissolves, 15 to 20 minutes. Stir in the kuzu root mixture and cook, stirring, until the mixture thickens, about 3 minutes. Spoon the filling evenly over the partially baked crust.

To make the topping: Cook the brown rice syrup in a small pot over high heat until it foams. Stir in the pecan pieces, then spoon the pecan mixture over the filling.

Bake for 30 minutes, or until the edges of the filling are set. The center will still be soft but will set as it cools. Cool completely before cutting into bars. These will keep, in a tightly sealed container, for 2 to 3 days.

SPICY APPLE-PEAR PIE

Autumn spells pie season to me. You can just smell the earthy spices and sweet fruit melting together in the oven, encased in a warm, flaky crust. Tree fruit, like apples and pears, are at their peak during late summer and autumn and provide us with a delicate, sweet, relaxing nature. Cooking them, especially baking, gentles the effect of their sugars on the bloodstream, creating a dessert that satisfies without making a mess of your blood chemistry.

Makes 8 to 10 servings

DOUBLE-CRUST PASTRY

2½ cups whole wheat pastry or sprouted whole wheat flour, plus more for rolling
½ cup avocado or extra-virgin olive oil
⅛ teaspoon sea salt
About 4 tablespoons chilled spring or filtered water

FILLING

3 to 4 medium-size ripe pears, peeled, cored, and thinly sliced
3 to 4 medium-size apples, peeled, cored, and thinly sliced
¼ cup Suzanne's Specialties brown rice syrup
2 tablespoons avocado or extra-virgin olive oil
3 tablespoons arrowroot powder
1 teaspoon ground ginger
Grated zest and juice of 1 lemon
Generous pinch each of ground cloves, ground nutmeg, and ground allspice

Place a rack in the center of the oven and preheat the oven to 325°F.

To make the pastry: In a bowl using a fork, two knives, or a pastry blender, combine the flour, oil, and salt until the mixture is the texture of wet sand. Slowly stir in enough water so the dough just gathers into a ball. Cover, and set aside 5 minutes to relax the gluten.

Divide the dough in half, then roll each piece between two sheets of parchment paper or on a dry, lightly floured work surface into a 10-inch circle. Gently fit one circle into a 9-inch pie plate. Pierce in several places with a fork.

To make the filling: Combine the pears, apples, brown rice syrup, oil, arrowroot powder, ginger, lemon zest and juice, cloves, nutmeg, and allspice in a large bowl. Spoon the filling into the pie shell, mounding the fruit in the center.

Gently place the remaining dough circle on top of the filling. Roll the edge of bottom crust up over the top crust and press the edges together to seal. Roll to the edge of the pan, and crimp decoratively to seal. Pierce the top crust in several places to allow steam to escape.

Bake for 45 to 60 minutes, or until the filling is bubbling and the crust is golden brown. Cool for 10 to 15 minutes before slicing, though longer is better so the filling sets up, as long as an hour. This will keep, in a tightly sealed container or tightly wrapped, for about 2 days.

BLUEBERRY GALETTE

This beautiful rustic tart makes a splendid ending to any summer meal. Filled to the brim with succulent, sweet berries, nestled in a free-form crust, this tart looks as casual as leisurely summer days. The cooling energy of blueberries is enhanced by the sparkling, fresh flavor of lemon.

Makes 8 to 10 servings

CRUST

2 cups whole wheat pastry or sprouted whole wheat flour, plus more for rolling

1 teaspoon baking powder

⅛ teaspoon sea salt

¼ cup avocado or extra-virgin olive oil

¼ to ½ cup spring or filtered water

BLUEBERRY FILLING

6 cups blueberries

4 tablespoons Suzanne's Specialties brown rice syrup

2 tablespoons arrowroot powder

2 teaspoons avocado or extra-virgin olive oil

Grated zest of 1 lemon

Juice of ½ lemon

GLAZE

½ cup Suzanne's Specialties brown rice syrup

2 teaspoons avocado or extra-virgin olive oil

Preheat the oven to 350°F. Line a 10-inch pizza pan with parchment paper or brush lightly with oil. (A lightly floured baking stone also works great with this recipe, but if you use the stone, preheat it for 30 minutes.)

To make the crust: Combine the flour, baking powder, and salt in a medium bowl. Stir in the oil until the mixture is the texture of wet sand. Mix in the water until the dough gathers into a ball. Roll out the dough between two sheets of parchment paper or on a dry, lightly floured surface into a 12-inch circle about ⅛ inch thick. Transfer the dough to the prepared pan or stone.

To make the filling: Combine the blueberries, brown rice syrup, arrowroot powder, oil, and lemon zest and juice in a large bowl and toss gently to coat the berries.

Spoon the filling into the center of the dough, leaving about 1 inch of dough exposed around the rim. Carefully fold the edges of the dough up over the filling, pinching to form pleats and leaving about a 5-inch opening in the center to expose the filling.

Bake for 30 to 35 minutes, or until the crust is golden brown and firm and the filling is bubbling. Remove from the oven and carefully transfer to a cooling rack.

To make the glaze: Combine the rice syrup and oil in a saucepan and cook over high heat until the mixture foams. Quickly brush over the crust to glaze. Cool completely before slicing. This will keep, in a tightly sealed container or tightly wrapped, for about 2 days.

CHOCOLATE BROWNIE CUPCAKES

I am not a fan of bananas in any way, shape, or form. They're too mushy and sweet for me . . . but that's a personal preference. In this recipe, I tried lots of things, from dates to applesauce to pumpkin, and even I had to admit that bananas produced the best texture and flavor.

Makes 6 to 8 cupcakes

CUPCAKES

⅔ cup mashed banana (from 1 to 2 ripe bananas)
½ cup Suzanne's Specialties Rice Mellow Crème
2 tablespoons coconut sugar
1 teaspoon pure vanilla extract
1¼ cups whole wheat pastry or sprouted whole wheat flour
4 tablespoons unsweetened cocoa powder
1 teaspoon baking powder
½ teaspoon baking soda
Pinch sea salt
Pinch ground cinnamon
½ cup Lily's Dark Chocolate Premium Baking Chips
½ to 1 cup spring or filtered water

VANILLA BUTTERCREME

1 cup Suzanne's Specialties Rice Mellow Crème
2 tablespoons vegan butter substitute
2 tablespoons vegan cream cheese substitute
1 teaspoon pure vanilla extract

Shaved Lily's chocolate or chocolate chips, for garnish

Preheat the oven to 350°F and line a muffin tin with paper liners (or use silicone cupcake cups).

To make the cupcakes: In a stand mixer (or using a hand mixer), whip together the mashed banana, Rice Mellow, coconut sugar, and vanilla until creamy. Mix in the flour, cocoa powder, baking powder, baking soda, salt, and cinnamon. Fold in the chocolate chips. Slowly add the water while mixing to create a thick, spoonable batter. Spoon the batter evenly into the cupcake liners, filling the cups two-thirds full.

Bake for 18 to 20 minutes, until the tops of the cupcakes spring back to the touch. Cool completely before frosting.

While the cupcakes bake, make the frosting: Using a hand mixer or whisk, whip the Rice Mellow, vegan butter, vegan cream cheese, and vanilla until smooth. Cover tightly and chill until ready to frost the cupcakes.

Spread frosting on top of each cupcake or use a piping bag and pipe the frosting onto each cupcake. Garnish with shaved chocolate or chocolate chips. These will keep, in a tightly sealed container, for 4 to 5 days.

ALMOND JOYFULS

These delightful treats were born of a craving for good ole Almond Joys, which I haven't eaten in years, but loved as a kid. And now I can love them again!

Makes 12 to 15 pieces

2 cups unsweetened shredded coconut

3 tablespoons Suzanne's Specialties brown rice syrup

2 tablespoons vegan butter substitute

Scant pinch sea salt

Scant pinch ground cinnamon

2 cups Lily's Dark Chocolate Premium Baking Chips, divided

12 to 15 whole almonds

Pulse the coconut, brown rice syrup, vegan butter, salt, and cinnamon in a food processor fitted with the metal blade until a sticky mixture forms that holds together.

Line a baking sheet with parchment paper. Using a mini ice cream scoop or 1-tablespoon measuring spoon, scoop the coconut mixture onto the prepared sheet. Chill in the fridge for 30 minutes, or until firmly set.

When the coconut is firm, melt the chocolate. Place the chocolate in a heat-resistant bowl over a pan of simmering water, taking care that the water doesn't touch the bottom of the pan. Stir gently until the chocolate melts and is smooth and creamy, 3 to 5 minutes.

Spoon the chocolate over each coconut mound, gently press a whole almond on top, and chill to set the chocolate.

COOK'S TIP: *If you are dealing with a nut allergy, you can use shredded coconut or a chocolate chip instead of topping with an almond.*

COOK'S TIP: *If you are not using Lily's, you will need to temper the chocolate. Melt 1½ cups chocolate in a double boiler or in a glass bowl over a pan of boiling water and stir until the chocolate melts and reaches 119°F on a candy thermometer. Remove from the heat, place on a dry towel (do not let the water touch the chocolate), and dry the bottom of the bowl. Stir in the remaining ½ cup chocolate until the temperature reduces to 86°F. Stir until smooth. Return the bowl over the boiling water and stir for 5 seconds. Remove to the towel and dry the bottom of the bowl.*

CANNOLI NAPOLEONS

This recipe was inspired by my friend and PBS colleague Lidia Bastianich. This fancy-looking dessert is so easy, you'll just love it! And mine has no refined sugar or saturated fat, so it's as good for you as it is yummy!

Makes 4 Napoleons

PASTRY

½ cup whole wheat pastry or sprouted whole wheat flour, plus more for rolling

¼ cup durum or semolina flour

1 tablespoon coconut sugar

⅛ teaspoon sea salt

¼ cup dry red wine, plus more as needed

1 tablespoon extra-virgin olive oil

½ teaspoon apple cider vinegar

CANNOLI CRÈME

1 (8-ounce) container vegan cream cheese substitute

5 ounces Suzanne's Specialties Rice Mellow Crème

2 teaspoons pure vanilla extract

3 ounces Lily's Dark Chocolate Premium Baking Chips

3 ounces slivered almonds

Non-GMO sunflower, safflower, or rice bran oil, for frying

CHOCOLATE SAUCE

⅓ cup unsweetened almond milk

2 tablespoons Suzanne's Specialties brown rice syrup

1 cup Lily's Dark Chocolate Premium Baking Chips

To make the pastry: Combine the flours, coconut sugar, and salt in the bowl of a food processor fitted with the metal blade and process just to mix. In a separate bowl, combine the wine, olive oil, and vinegar. With the processor running, slowly pour the wine mixture into the feed tube until the dough gathers on the blade. It should be soft and tender, just gathered together, so you may need more wine. Transfer the dough to a lightly floured surface and knead by hand into a soft, smooth ball, 1 to 2 minutes. Flatten into a disk, wrap very tightly in plastic, and refrigerate. You can make the dough up to 2 days in advance.

To make the cannoli crème: In a bowl with a hand mixer or whisk, whip the vegan cream cheese, Rice Mellow, and vanilla until creamy. Chill completely before use. When ready to assemble the Napoleons, fold the chocolate chips and almonds into the mixture.

Line a baking sheet with parchment and lightly flour the paper.

On a lightly floured surface, roll out the dough into a rectangle about 14 by 11 inches. With a sharp knife, trim the edges and divide the rectangle into 12 squares, about 3½ inches on a side. Set the squares on the prepared baking sheet to rest for 15 minutes before frying.

To fry the pastry, pour ¼ inch of oil into a deep skillet and heat over medium heat. With a fork, pierce each pastry square all over the surface to prevent the pastry from bubbling when frying. Heat the oil until a small piece of dough sizzles gently when placed into it. Lay in as many squares as you can in the hot oil about 2 inches apart. Raise the heat to medium-high to keep the oil temperature up. Fry the squares for about 3 minutes on each side, occasionally pushing them under the oil to heat the top surface. As the tops begin to bubble, press with tongs to prevent big bubbles from bursting. When the bottom is golden brown, flip the squares over and fry until evenly colored and crisp on both sides.

Lift the squares carefully from the oil with tongs and allow excess oil to drip off. Transfer them to drain on parchment paper, flipping them over to blot the oil from both sides. Repeat with all the pastry squares, allowing the oil to reheat in between batches and adding oil as needed.

To make the chocolate sauce: Heat the milk and syrup in a pot to a high rolling boil. Pour over the chocolate chips in a heat-resistant bowl and whisk until smooth.

Assemble your Napoleons shortly before serving, with 3 squares for each one. Set one square on a plate; dollop about 1½ tablespoons of cannoli crème in the center; lay another square on top and press gently to spread the cream. Dollop on another layer of crème, cover with the third square, and press gently. Drizzle with the chocolate sauce and serve immediately.

RECOMMENDED READING

The following volumes have become invaluable to me over the years and I look to them (and many others) constantly for inspiration and to further my understanding of the laws of nature. My gratitude to all the authors for their wisdom.

Annemarie Colbin, *The Natural Gourmet* (New York: Ballantine, 1989)

Steve Gagné, *Energetics of Food* (New Mexico: Spiral Science, 1990)

Michio and Aveline Kushi, *Macrobiotic Diet* (New York: Japan Publications, 1985)

Michio Kushi, *Your Face Never Lies* (New Jersey: Avery, 1983)

Michio Kushi, *How to See Your Health* (New York: Japan Publications, 1985)

Michio Kushi, *Nine Star Ki* (Massachusetts: One Peaceful World, 1995)

Georges Ohsawa, *You Are All Sanpaku* (New York: Citadel, 1965)

Jon Sandifer, *Feng Shui Astrology* (New York: Ballantine, 1997)

William Tara, *The Magic Mirror* (Boston: Self-Pub, 1984)

William Tara, *Natural Body, Natural Mind* (Philadelphia: X-Libris, 2008)

Ilza Veith, *The Yellow Emperor's Classic of Internal Medicine* (California: University of California, 1949)

RESOURCES

For more information and recipes, as well as links to useful products and services, visit christinacooks.com.

ACKNOWLEDGMENTS

No one does what they do without the support and love of others. The saying that no one is an island couldn't be truer in my case. I have a posse of people to thank; some of them have been with me for ages and some are new to my world. All of them make me a better person, teacher, and proactivist.

I have to thank all my students, who over the years have taught me so many valuable lessons, from really hearing what people are saying, to giving people what they need, to always being open and generous with what I perceive to be the truth, to teaching me how to communicate so I can help them discover their paths to wellness.

To my teachers, including Michio Kushi and Bill Tara, who mentored me into finding my voice and my way of communicating, for their encouragement and generosity of spirit.

I have to thank my friends or, as I like to call them, my chosen family, for the unconditional love and support they give me. My circle is small but mighty. Eric and Madinad, Cynthia and Dennis, Sue and David, Michele and Kevin, Lenore and Robb, Kimmie and Jimmie, Amy, Molly, Mary, Patrecia, Lisa, Elisabetta, Tony 2 Toes, Susan M., Shannon, Alex, Ben, Sara, Jenn, John, Anthony, Kay and Jean (not only my dear friend, but also my qigong *sifu* who saved my back, literally), the Triplets, little Jen, Carly and Ally, Gillian, Heather and Cosimo, Carol, Dale and Angel, Frankie O, Uncle Sandy, Lorenzo and Randall.

To my fit family at Fitness Works: Joanne, you and your crew kept me sane (and strong) when I could not read, write, or test one more recipe!

I'd be remiss if I didn't mention my older brother, Tom, whose wisdom I have tapped many times. And my sister-in-law, Megan, whom I just adore, along with my niece, Olivia.

My mother taught me everything I wanted to be and everything I didn't and for that I am grateful.

To my dad, who thinks I can do no wrong: thank you.

To my team at BenBella Books—Glenn, Leah, Adrienne, Sarah, Alicia, Rachel, Anika, Jessika, Heather, Erica, and Lindsay—who took me on and nurtured this project with love and enthusiasm: I can't thank you enough. I hope this is the start of a long and beautiful relationship. Special thanks to Trish Malone, whose mindful editing took this information and molded it into the book you hold. Everyone at BenBella, from design to marketing, has been sensitive, open-minded, and a true pleasure to work with on this project. A powerful team of (mostly) women!

To Maja Pecanic-Danica for her luscious photography and Vlatka for her loving preparation of my recipes. And to Jadranka, Zlatko, and Marina for introducing me to both of these powerful and talented women. And to Cynthia and Susan, without whose support the gorgeous photos would not have been created.

My grandfather would be so proud that his humble cutting board became the catalyst for this work and for so much of what I do in life. Pop, I think of you every day. I miss you and wish you were here.

And then there's my North Star, my compass and guiding light, Robert, the heart of my heart and partner in this life. You complete me.

METRIC CONVERSIONS

ABBREVIATION KEY

tsp = teaspoon
tbsp = tablespoon
dsp = dessert spoon

U.S. STANDARD	U.K.
¼ tsp	¼ tsp (scant)
½ tsp	½ tsp (scant)
¾ tsp	½ tsp (rounded)
1 tsp	¾ tsp (slightly rounded)
1 tbsp	2½ tsp
¼ cup	¼ cup minus 1 dsp
⅓ cup	¼ cup plus 1 tsp
½ cup	⅓ cup plus 2 dsp
⅔ cup	½ cup plus 1 tbsp
¾ cup	½ cup plus 2 tbsp
1 cup	¾ cup and 2 dsp

RECIPE INDEX